WHAT
COMES BEFORE
PHONICS?

Sara Miller McCune founded SAGE Publishing in 1965 to support the dissemination of usable knowledge and educate a global community. SAGE publishes more than 1000 journals and over 800 new books each year, spanning a wide range of subject areas. Our growing selection of library products includes archives, data, case studies and video. SAGE remains majority owned by our founder and after her lifetime will become owned by a charitable trust that secures the company's continued independence.

Los Angeles | London | New Delhi | Singapore | Washington DC | Melbourne

SALLY NEAUM

WHAT COMES BEFORE PHONICS?

Learning Matters
An imprint of SAGE Publications Ltd
1 Oliver's Yard
55 City Road
London EC1Y 1SP

SAGE Publications Inc.
2455 Teller Road
Thousand Oaks, California 91320

SAGE Publications India Pvt Ltd
B 1/I 1 Mohan Cooperative Industrial Area
Mathura Road
New Delhi 110 044

SAGE Asia-Pacific Pte Ltd
3 Church Street
#10–04 Samsung Hub
Singapore 049483

Editor: Amy Thornton
Development editor: Geoff Barker
Production controller: Chris Marke
Project management: Deer Park Productions
Marketing manager: Catherine Slinn
Cover design: Wendy Scott
Typeset by: C&M Digitals (P) Ltd, Chennai, India
Printed in the UK

Published in 2017 by Learning Matters Ltd.
© 2017 Sally Neaum

Library of Congress Control Number: 2016954951

British Library Cataloguing in Publication Data

A catalogue record for this book is available from the British Library.

ISBN: 978-1-4739-6849-3 (pbk)
ISBN: 978-1-4739-6848-6 (hbk)

At SAGE we take sustainability seriously. Most of our products are printed in the UK using FSC papers and boards. When we print overseas we ensure sustainable papers are used as measured by the PREPS grading system. We undertake an annual audit to monitor our sustainability.

Contents

The author   vi

Acknowledgements   vii

Introduction   1

1   Early literacy: the current context   11

2   Leading into literacy   30

3   Speaking and listening   49

4   Physical foundations of literacy   74

5   Metalinguistic development   90

6   Print awareness   105

7   Symbolising and representation   128

8   Phonological awareness   140

Conclusion   157

Index   162

The author

Sally Neaum is a lecturer in education. She teaches on a number of undergraduate and postgraduate programmes and is an academic supervisor at master's and doctoral level. She has worked as a nursery and primary school teacher, an early years and inclusion advisory teacher, and in initial teacher training. Her current area of research is children's engagement with literacy practices.

Acknowledgements

Every effort has been made to trace the copyright holders and to obtain their permission for the use of copyright material. The publisher and author will gladly receive any information enabling them to rectify any error or omission in subsequent editions.

Introduction

Becoming literate

Being literate has a powerful impact on children's learning in school and beyond. There is, therefore, a strong emphasis on literacy in children's early schooling. Becoming proficient in phonics has been shown to be an important part of becoming literate, and teaching phonics is now strongly embedded in early literacy teaching in schools and early years settings. Phonics teaching is a well-documented process, and there is a significant body of literature, and many professional development opportunities, to enable teachers and practitioners to become proficient teachers of phonics.

However, despite this focus on phonics in the early years there are, it seems, far fewer opportunities to become knowledgeable about what comes before the formal teaching of phonics. What should we be focusing on in a child's earliest years? What do children need to know and experience to enable them to access phonics teaching with success?

Additionally, in recent years, there has been a persistent pull towards teaching phonics at an increasingly earlier age, using a teacher-led formal approach. We know that this is not appropriate for many young children. However, without an understanding of the ways in which certain knowledge and understanding lead into phonics, it is difficult for early years teachers and practitioners to justify and implement a different approach.

However, before we consider what comes before phonics, it is important to understand why literacy is so important and the role of phonics in becoming literate.

Why is it important to become literate?

Becoming and being literate is usually associated with schooling. It is something that usually happens at school and forms the basis of education. However, being literate is significantly more important than just as a tool for school-based learning: being literate is fundamental to our engagement and enjoyment in life. It is a skill that broadens and deepens our experiences across our lives and, as such, is a vital skill to acquire and develop.

Being literate opens up a world of richness, enjoyment and knowledge. It enables us to go beyond our own experiences and enter the experiences of others. Being literate means that we have access to the thoughts, feelings, perceptions, knowledge and expertise of other people, across time and space. In addition, it enables us to form and maintain relationships, communicate our own thoughts and ideas, express the richness of our imagination and convey our knowledge and understanding, all of which contribute significantly to the quality, enjoyment and engagement in our lives.

Being literate also enables us to participate fully in society. Flewitt (2013) argues that it is a platform for individuals to develop their knowledge and fully participate in society through oral, written, printed and digital media. UNESCO similarly recognises that literacy (defined as the ability to identify, understand, interpret, create, communicate, compute and use printed materials associated with varying contexts) acts as an instrument of participation and empowerment, essential to social and human development (UNESCO, in Flewitt, 2013).

Literacy also lies at the heart of education (Flewitt, 2013) and therefore has a significant impact on subsequent opportunities in life (National Literacy Trust (NLT), 2012). The NLT reports that one in six people in the United Kingdom lives with poor literacy skills.

> Without good reading, writing and communication skills a child won't be able to succeed at school and as a young adult they will be locked out of the job market. They will be unable to reach their full potential or make a valuable contribution to the economic and cultural life of our nation. Their poor literacy skills will also affect them as parents as they will struggle to support their child's learning and generations of families will be locked in poverty and social exclusion.
>
> (National Literacy Trust, 2012, p3)

Becoming literate is therefore vital, and schools have the responsibility to ensure that children become literate. However, this is not a straightforward issue. Despite agreement about the importance of literacy, how schools achieve this is the subject of considerable debate and tension – in particular, how and when phonics should be part of the process of learning to read and spell. These issues are discussed in depth in Chapter 1 but, as a context for understanding what comes before phonics, it is important to understand what phonics is and what we know about the place of phonics in becoming literate.

What is phonics?

Phonics is a way of teaching reading that emphasises the acquisition of letter–sound correspondence as the basis of teaching children to read and spell. The primary focus of phonics is to ensure that, as children move into becoming conventionally literate, they understand how letters (graphemes) are linked to sounds (phonemes), and how to blend phonemes together into words and segment words in phonemes. This enables children to decode text and supports spelling.

In England, the mandated approach is one termed 'systematic synthetic phonics'. It is *systematic* in that the sounds and skills are taught explicitly and directly in a deliberate, planned sequence, and *synthetic* in the requirement that children synthesise (blend) sounds together.

Systematic synthetic phonics

Spoken words and written words

Language is made up of words. Words are made up of sounds (phonemes). When we write, we use written symbols (graphemes) to represent the sounds. These graphemes may be single letters or combinations of letters such as *sh*, *oy* and *igh*. Once we know how these grapheme–phoneme correspondences (GPCs) work, we can encode spoken words in writing for others to read, and we can decode words that others have written.

Synthetic phonics

The *synthetic* part of the term 'synthetic phonics' comes from the part played by synthesising (blending) in reading as outlined below. Children are taught GPCs and how to use this knowledge to work out words from the beginning, starting at the simplest level.

- For reading, children are taught to look at the letters from left to right, convert them into sounds and blend (synthesise) the sounds to work out the spoken forms of the words. For example, if children see the word 'hat', they need to know what sound to say for each grapheme (/h/ - /a/ - /t/) and then to be able to blend those sounds together into a recognisable word. Once words have been read this way often enough (and this can vary from child to child), they become known, and the words can then be read without sounding out and blending.

- For spelling, children are taught to segment spoken words into sounds and write down graphemes for those sounds. For example, if children want to write 'hat', then they need to be able to split it into the sounds /h/ - /a/ - /t/ and write the appropriate letters (TDA, 2011).

The place of phonics in becoming literate

The overall consensus is that the systematic teaching of phonics has an essential part to play in children becoming literate. Major studies conclude that phonics is an important aspect of learning to read, but it is insufficient on its own as a way to teach children to read effectively with understanding and enjoyment.

A number of large-scale studies, including national reports and meta-analyses of existing evidence, have drawn this conclusion. Adams (1990) explored the most efficient and effective ways to teach reading and asked the question 'Why phonics?' in learning to read, and concluded that *students must appreciate the alphabetic principle to become proficient readers: they must acquire a sense of the correspondences between letters and sounds upon which it is based* (Adams, 1990, p29). However, she cautions that *necessary* is not the same as *sufficient,* and that to become skilful readers, children need more than just an understanding of the alphabetic principle. Similarly, the National Reading Panel (NICHD, 2006) in their report *Teaching Children* to *Read* found from their meta-analysis of research evidence that phonics instruction had significant benefits for children learning to read but warned that while phonics skills are necessary in order to learn to read, they are not sufficient in their own right: that phonics skills must be integrated with the development of phonemic awareness, fluency and text reading comprehension skills. More recently, Torgerson *et al.* (2006) also concluded that there is evidence to suggest that systematic phonics should be a routine part of literacy teaching, and that all teachers should have this in their repertoire of pedagogical skills. However, they also conclude that this should be with a *broad literacy curriculum* (Torgerson *et al.*, 2006, p10). Most recently, the Education Endowment Foundation (EEF) stated that

> *Phonics approaches have been consistently found to be effective in supporting younger readers to master the basics of reading. ... Research suggests that phonics is particularly beneficial for younger learners (4–7 year olds) as they begin to read.*

(EEF, 2015)

And, in line with other large-scale studies on phonics teaching, they caution that

> *effective phonics techniques are usually embedded in a rich literacy environment for early readers and are only one part of a successful literacy strategy.*

WHAT DOES RESEARCH TELL US?

A systematic review of the research literature on the use of phonics in the teaching of reading and spelling (Torgerson *et al.*, 2006).

The Universities of York and Sheffield were commissioned by the Department for Education and Skills (DfES) to conduct a systematic review of experimental research on the use of phonics in the teaching of reading and spelling. The review entailed a systematic review of existing research. This means that explicit methods were used to identify, select and include studies that fitted pre-specified criteria. This included that the studies were randomised controlled trials (RCTs). Ben Goldacre (2013) described RCTs in education.

> *We simply take a group of children, or schools; we split them into two groups at random; we give one intervention to one group, and the other intervention to the other group; then we measure how each group is doing, to see if one intervention achieved its supposed outcome any better.*

(Goldacre, 2013)

The aims of the review were to investigate and compare the effectiveness of different approaches to the initial teaching of reading and spelling. The review questions were as follows.

(Continued)

- How effective are different approaches to phonics teaching in comparison to each other, including the specific area of *analytic* versus *synthetic* phonics?

- How do different approaches impact on the application of phonics in reading and writing, including beyond the early years?

- Is there a need to differentiate between phonics for reading and phonics for spelling?

- What proportion of literacy teaching should be based on the use of phonics?

The review drew a series of conclusions, which resulted in recommendations for teaching, teacher training and research.

Teaching

- Systematic phonics instruction should be part of every literacy teacher's repertoire and a routine part of literacy teaching.

- Teachers who do not use systematic phonics in their teaching should add it to their routine practices.

- Systematic phonics should be used both with normally developing children and those at risk of failure.

Teacher training

- The evidence implies that learning to use systematic phonics in a judicious balance with other elements should form a part of every literacy teacher's training. However:

   o There was no strong RCT evidence that one system of systematic phonics was more effective than another.

   o There was no strong RCT evidence on how much systematic phonics is needed.

   o Evidence was insufficient as to whether or not phonics teaching boosts comprehension, and whether or not phonics should be used to teach spelling.

Research

A large-scale UK-based cluster-randomised controlled trial would enable further investigation of the relative effectiveness of different types of phonics instruction for children with different learning characteristics.

Phonics and children who have English as an additional language (EAL)

Becoming literate, and having access to all the delights, enjoyment and engagement in education and society it brings is vital for all children, including those who have English as an additional language (EAL). In the United Kingdom, the number of children who speak one or more languages in addition to English has increased significantly over the past few years. The 2013 school census showed that there are more than a million children between the ages of 5 and 16 years in UK schools who speak in excess of 360 languages between them in addition to English (NALDIC, 2015; Strand *et al.*, 2015).

Being bilingual or multilingual has significant advantages (Byers-Heinlein and Lew-Williams, 2013). Living in more than one language offers children first-hand experience and understanding about language, and about societies and cultures. Being bilingual extends language capacity, both language for communication and language for thinking. To be able to use different languages brings a wider capacity for understanding and expressing thoughts and ideas, the potential for a more nuanced vocabulary, and it enables different ways of interacting and communicating across societies and cultures. Being bilingual has been shown to enhance metalinguistic awareness: an awareness of, and knowledge about, language (Bialystok, 1978) (*see* Chapter 5), and phonological processing (Monaghan, 2014) (*see* Chapter 8).

Phonics has been shown to be *necessary but not sufficient* for children with EAL becoming literate in English. To read and understand a text requires children to both decode words and comprehend the meaning of the text. Phonics only enables decoding; it doesn't enable comprehension of a text, and it is this aspect of reading that it is suggested has an impact on the reading ability of children with EAL (Stuart, 2004). Stuart (2004) suggests that possibly the underdeveloped oral language abilities of children with EAL delays development of their ability to read and understand continuous text. Therefore, a focus on oral language development and comprehension, and reading comprehension as well as phonics, is likely to offer children the best chance of success.

We can, therefore, conclude that current evidence about the place of phonics in becoming literate, both for children with English as a first language and those who have English as an additional language, is that it is *necessary but not sufficient*. Children need other knowledge, skills and experiences if they are going to be able to read with understanding and enjoyment. The debates about the balance between phonics and the development of other knowledge, skills and experience in teaching children to read are significant and ongoing (for example, *see* the poet Michael Rosen's blog). In addition, there are also significant ongoing debates within phonics teaching about what the approach should be. Unresolved questions and issues include the following.

- What is an appropriate balance between a focus on decoding (phonics) and a focus on comprehension?
- Which phonics approach is most beneficial to the majority of children?
- Which group of children benefits from which approach?
- Whose learning is limited by particular approaches?
- At what age and/or stage should phonics teaching take place?
- What age- and stage-related expectations are appropriate for stated curriculum aims?

- How should we assess children's phonics learning?

- What should the content of teacher training and early years practitioner training be to ensure that they are equipped to meet all children's literacy needs?

- What is the role of policy and political rhetoric in teaching reading?

- Which research approach is best placed to inform our understanding of phonics teaching in schools?

- How do we translate research evidence into effective school-based practice?

DEVELOP YOUR UNDERSTANDING

The questions and issues listed above show areas of contention and debate, and there is considerable material documenting the different views and approaches. Develop your understanding of these debates by considering these different views.

A good starting point is the parliamentary education committee web forum. Views on the strength of evidence for the current government policy on phonics were requested, and a range of views, many supported by research evidence, were submitted.

www.parliament.uk/business/committees/committees-a-z/commons-select/education-committee/dfe-evidence-check-forum/phonics/

Other websites and blogs that express different views about the place of phonics in literacy teaching and learning that you could explore are:

- Too Much, Too Soon;

- Reading Reform Foundation;

- United Kingdom Literacy Association.

See also:

Goouch, K and Lambrith, A (2016) *Teaching Early Reading and Phonics: Creative Approaches to Early Literacy* (2nd Ed). London: SAGE.

Johnson, R and Watson, J (2014) *Teaching Synthetic Phonics in Primary School* (2nd edn). London: SAGE.

What comes before phonics?

Phonics is therefore one part of becoming conventionally literate – necessary, but not sufficient. It is, therefore, important that all children come to phonics learning with a good chance of succeeding *and* with a range of other knowledge, skills and experiences that enable them to move into becoming literate with relative ease and with enjoyment.

This book looks in detail at the knowledge, understanding, skills and attitudes that children need to come to phonics teaching – ready to learn and with a high chance of success. The focus of the book is young children who do not have learning difficulties, including the specific learning difficulty, dyslexia. These are more specialist areas, and although some of the content of the book may be relevant, the more individual needs of these children will require additional consideration. There is a significant body of literature and organisations and services that can support you in meeting these children's needs as they move into becoming literate.

This book discusses the knowledge, skills and understandings necessary for what comes *before* phonics. It creates a framework for developing appropriate provision for children in the earliest stages of becoming literate. This is important. Becoming literate is a fluid and dynamic process, not a strict linear, hierarchical process. The ideas in this book are drawn from a range of fields and bring together what is known about early experiences that enable children to access phonics teaching successfully. It is not a curriculum for early literacy, nor a prescribed set of outcomes to be listed and 'ticked off'. In writing the book, I began with the premise that it is important to understand *why* children need this range of knowledge and skills, not just *what* they need. Therefore, the book draws on, and outlines, evidence that informs our understanding of effective provision and practice for what comes before phonics. The aim is for students and people working in early years to recognise aspects of early years practice that anticipate phonics teaching, and to label them as such within their professional knowledge and in their planning for continuous and enhanced provision. My best hope is that this knowledge and understanding will enable early years staff to develop practice in early years that resists the current 'push down' of formal teaching: that practitioners' enhanced professional understanding will lead to effective provision that reflects what we know about how young children learn and what comes before phonics.

Chapter 1 outlines the current context of early literacy teaching. It considers the current approach to teaching reading at Foundation Stage and Key Stage One. The chapter outlines what we know about how very young children learn and identifies tensions between a formal approach to phonics teaching and young children's learning, including the current debates around school readiness.

Chapter 2 explores the early interactions and experiences that lead into literacy. It considers the role of adults in facilitating these experiences and interactions at home and in early years settings. The chapter looks at effective pre-school provision to support literacy.

Chapters 3–8 each consider one aspect of what comes before phonics. It is important to be aware that the knowledge, skills, understandings and experiences outlined happen as part of young children's active integrated learning, not separately as they are described in the book. They are described in this discrete way for ease of understanding, but need to be applied to what we know about how young children learn.

Chapter 3 considers the basis of all learning: speaking and listening. It explains how children acquire and develop language. Language learning for children growing up learning more than one language is also considered. The chapter outlines the role of adults in supporting children's language acquisition and development, including the importance of engaging children with books, songs, rhymes, poems and language play. Ways to support and encourage parents to talk and read with their children are discussed.

Chapter 4 looks at the importance of physical activity that supports sensory awareness and integration, with a particular focus on literacy learning. The most important messages in this chapter are that children's physical development is integral to learning, and that young children do not learn to sit still by sitting still.

Chapter 5 discusses the importance of meta-cognitive and meta-linguistic awareness. It considers why this is important for literacy learning, including phonics.

Chapter 6 discusses print awareness. It considers what we mean by forms and functions of print and how children learn about these in a meaningful way. The importance of these understandings to literacy learning is discussed.

Chapter 7 discusses the role of symbolising and representation in becoming literate, and how this leads into phonics. It considers how children learn to symbolise.

Chapter 8 considers phonological awareness. It explains what is meant by phonological awareness, including phonemic awareness, and how this leads into phonics.

Finally, throughout this book it will be stressed that orally sounding out phonemes, identifying phoneme–grapheme correspondence and modelling how to blend and segment words in context and as appropriate, is an important aspect of what comes before phonics. Children whose early experiences include an awareness of these building blocks of phonics are likely to come to the later formal phonics teaching with a high chance of success.

References

Adams, MJ (1990) *Beginning to Read: Thinking and Learning about Print*. London: MIT Press.

Bialystok, E (1987) Influences of bilingualism on metalinguistic development. *Second Language Research* 3(2): 154–66.

Byers-Heinlein, K and Lew-Williams, C (2013) *Bilingualism in the Early Years: What the Science Says*. Available online at: www.learninglandscapes.ca/images/documents/ll-no13/byers-heinlein.pdf (accessed 11 September 2016).

Education Endowment Foundation (EEF) (2015) Phonics. Available online at: https://educationendowmentfoundation.org.uk/toolkit/toolkit-a-z/phonics/ (accessed 11 September 2016).

Flewitt, R (2013) Early literacy: a broader vision (TACTYC). Available online at: http://eprints.ncrm.ac.uk/3132/1/flewitt_occasional-paper3.pdf (accessed 11 September 2016).

Goldacre, B (2013) Teachers! What would evidence based practice look like? Available online at: www.badscience.net/2013/03/heres-my-paper-on-evidence-and-teaching-for-the-education-minister/ (accessed 11 September 2016).

Monaghan, F (2014) EAL – Testing the limits of phonics. NASSEA conference, 2014. Available online at: www.nassea.org.uk/userfiles/file/EAL_Testing_the_limits_of_phonics.pdf (accessed 11 September 2016).

NALDIC (2015) Research and statistics. Available online at: www.naldic.org.uk/research-and-information/ (accessed 11 September 2016).

National Literacy Trust (NLT) (2013) Words for life. Available online at: **www.literacytrust.org.uk/assets/0001/4600/Impact_report_2011-12.pdf** (accessed 11 September 2016).

NICHD (2006) Teaching children to read. Report of the National Reading Panel: Findings and determinations. Available online at: **www.nichd.nih.gov/publications/pubs/nrp/Pages/findings.aspx** (accessed 11 September 2016).

Rosen, M (2013) Phonics: A summary of my views. Available online at: **http://michaelrosenblog.blogspot.co.uk/2013/01/phonics-summary-of-my-views.html** (accessed 11 September 2016).

Strand, S, Malmberg, L and Hall, J (2015) English as an additional language (EAL) and educational achievement in England: An analysis of the National Pupil Database. Available online at: **https://educationendowmentfoundation.org.uk/uploads/pdf/EAL_and_educational_achievement2.pdf** (accessed 11 September 2016).

Stuart, M (2004) Getting ready for reading: A follow-up study of inner city second language learners at the end of Key Stage 1. *British Journal of Educational Psychology* 74: 15–36.

TDA (2011) Systematic synthetic phonics in initial teaching training: Guidance and support materials. 2011 notes issued to ITT providers by TDA. London: DFE.

Torgerson, C, Brooks, G and Hall, J (2006) A systematic review of the research literature on the use of phonics in the teaching of reading and spelling. Available online at: **http://dera.ioe.ac.uk/14791/1/RR711_.pdf** (accessed 11 September 2016).

Websites

Too Much, Too Soon campaign
www.toomuchtoosoon.org/ (accessed 11 September 2016).

United Kingdom Literacy Association
https://ukla.org/news/story/new_presentation_on_phonics_and_raising_standards_of_literacy (accessed 11 September 2016).

Reading Reform Foundation
www.rrf.org.uk/ (accessed 11 September 2016).

1 Early literacy: the current context

Introduction

Being literate has a profound impact on children's learning throughout their education, so learning to read is an important focus in children's earliest years at school. Approaches to teaching reading have changed over time. In the 1980s, there was a period termed the 'reading wars' in which there was intense debate about how to approach teaching young children to read: a whole word approach or a phonics approach?

However, since the Rose Review of reading in 2006, there has been a strong shift towards a single approach to teaching reading using systematic synthetic phonics. This approach begins in the Early Years Foundation Stage and is a significant part of the current focus on school readiness. There are, however, concerns that the introduction of a more formal, teacher-led, content-based approach in early years is not appropriate for many Foundation Stage children.

This chapter considers the current approach to teaching reading at Foundation Stage and Key Stage 1, in particular the strong emphasis on systematic synthetic phonics. It considers children who are learning English as an additional language and learning to read. The chapter outlines our understanding about how very young children learn, and discusses the tensions between the required more formal approach to phonics teaching and young children's learning. It emphasises the importance of professional knowledge about the teaching of reading, including what comes before formal teaching of phonics, so that as teachers and practitioners we are able to make developmentally appropriate provision for all children, including our youngest children and children who are not yet ready for formal phonics teaching.

The current approach to teaching reading at Foundation Stage and Key Stage 1

The requirements for teaching reading at Foundation Stage and Key Stage 1 are clear and explicit: children should be taught to read using systematic synthetic phonics. This is a requirement for all settings and schools, mandated by the government who state that they will *ensure that all children have the chance to follow an enriching curriculum by getting them reading early. That means supporting the teaching of systematic synthetic phonics.*

(DFE, 2010, p44)

Systematic synthetic phonics

Spoken words and written words

Language is made up of words. Words are made up of sounds (phonemes). When we write, we use written symbols (graphemes) to represent the sounds. These graphemes may be single letters or combinations of letters such as *sh*, *oy* and *igh*. Once we know how these grapheme–phoneme correspondences (GPCs) work, we can encode spoken words in writing for others to read, and we can decode words that others have written.

Synthetic phonics

The *synthetic* part of the term 'synthetic phonics' comes from the part played by synthesising (blending) in reading, as outlined below. Children are taught GPCs and how to use this knowledge to work words out from the beginning, starting at the simplest level.

- For reading, children are taught to look at the letters from left to right, convert them into sounds and blend (synthesise) the sounds to work out the spoken forms of the words. For example, if children see the word 'hat', they need to know what sound to say for each grapheme (/h/ - /a/ - /t/) and then to be able to blend those sounds together into a recognisable word. Once words have been read this way often enough (and this can vary from child to child), they become known and can then be read without sounding out and blending.

- For spelling, children are taught to segment spoken words into sounds and write down graphemes for those sounds. For example, if children want to write 'hat', then they need to be able to split it into the sounds /h/ - /a/ - /t/ and write the appropriate letters (TDA, 2011).

To ascertain the phonics knowledge that children have acquired during Foundation Stage and early Key Stage 1, alongside the requirement to teach reading using systematic synthetic phonics, a phonics screening check for six-year-old children has been introduced with the stated aim of assessing whether or not *children have mastered the basic skills of early reading* and to ensure that children with learning difficulties in this area can be identified (DFE, 2010, p44).

In addition to mandating this approach to teaching reading, and to ensure that this approach becomes embedded in schools and settings, the Teachers' Standards (2011) (the stated minimum requirements for teachers' practice and conduct) now also include explicit reference to trainees developing the knowledge and skill to be able to teach reading using systematic synthetic phonics. They state that all teachers, including trainee teachers, must

- demonstrate an understanding of and take responsibility for promoting high standards of literacy, articulacy and the correct use of standard English, whatever the teacher's specialist subject

- if teaching early reading, demonstrate a clear understanding of systematic synthetic phonics (DFE, 2011, p1).

Similarly, the Early Years Teacher Standards (DFE/NCTL, 2013, p3) state that teachers in early years must *demonstrate a clear understanding of systematic synthetic phonics in the teaching of early reading.*

The extent to which schools and organisations involved in teacher training comply with these requirements are now part of education accountability structures. School OFSTED (Office for Standards in Education) inspections have a strong focus on teaching reading using this approach and, in addition, a significant aspect of OFSTED inspections of university providers of teacher training is to ensure how confidently and competently trainees teach systematic synthetic phonics in the classroom, and the quality of the training that they receive to enable them to do this (Ellis and Moss, 2013).

The requirements to teach reading using systematic synthetic phonics are thus explicit at all levels of provision and accountability. Schools and settings must have the skill, knowledge and resources to teach reading using this approach, and are held accountable for doing so.

Why this approach to teaching reading?

The genesis of this powerfully mandated approach to teaching reading is the Rose Review (2006). Rose's *Independent review of the teaching of early reading* (2006) was established in response to concerns about the apparent lack of progress in raising standards of reading, despite the introduction of the National Curriculum in 1989, and in anticipation of what was then the forthcoming Early Years Foundation Stage. Among other aspects of reading, the review was explicitly asked to consider best practice in the teaching of early reading and synthetic phonics. Rose's work drew on evidence from both research and practice, in particular a study conducted in Clackmannanshire in Scotland (Johnson and Watson, 2005). This study claimed to have shown that children taught using synthetic phonics had made significant gains in contrast to children taught to read in different ways, and these conclusions were particularly influential in informing Rose's conclusions and recommendations.

The review's conclusions were accepted by government and have subsequently informed policy. With regard to the current policy on using systematic synthetic phonics to teach reading, Rose's influence is clear. The review recommended that

> *despite uncertainties in research findings, the practice seen by the review shows that the systematic approach, which is generally understood as 'synthetic' phonics, offers the vast majority of young children the best and most direct route to becoming skilled readers and writers.*

(Rose, 2006, p5)

In addition, Rose also concluded that their recommended approach to teaching reading should be underpinned by the *simple view of reading* which, in addition to a systematic approach to teaching phonics, requires provision for young children's literacy learning to *be set within a broad and rich language curriculum* (Rose, 2006, p71).

The Simple View of Reading

The Simple View of Reading is a conceptual framework that contends that there are two essential aspects of learning to read that come together to enable a child to read fluently and with understanding: word recognition processes and language comprehension. (A simple view of writing has also been developed (Phonics International, 2012) which demonstrates the role of phonics in writing. This is not discussed here.)

The Simple View of Reading shows that both word recognition processes and language comprehension need to be developed and nurtured as children become readers. Word recognition processes involve a child learning the alphabetic principle: the ability to segment spoken words into their constituent phonemes; knowledge of grapheme–phoneme correspondences (phonic knowledge); and the ability to blend phonemes into words (Rose, 2006, p125). However, this ability to decode words is not sufficient in itself; reading also involves the ability to comprehend the meaning of the text. Reading comprehension is underpinned by language comprehension, so, in addition to good word recognition skills, a child needs strong oral language and comprehension skills to become a good reader. The Simple View of Reading depicts the interrelationship between these two vital dimensions of effective reading.

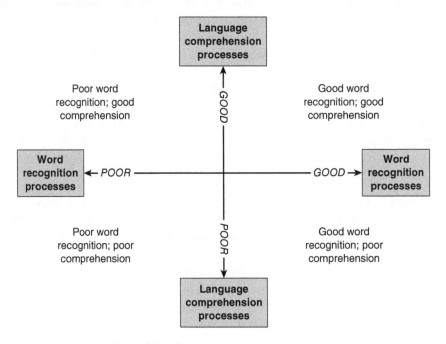

Figure 1.1   The Simple View of Reading

Children in the top-right quadrant of the framework have good word recognition and language comprehension skills: they can both decode text and comprehend what they have read, and are therefore likely to be good readers. The other three quadrants in the framework highlight predicted patterns of poor reading.

- In the bottom-right quadrant are children who can decode words with relative ease but have poor comprehension skills so are likely to have difficulties understanding what they have read.

- In the top-left quadrant are children who have difficulty with word recognition, although their language comprehension skills are sound. This lack of ability to decode acts as a barrier to accessing written text.

- In the bottom-left quadrant are the children who have difficulties with both dimensions of reading: word recognition and language comprehension. These children are likely to be poor readers.

Therefore, the current requirement for teaching reading at Foundation Stage and Key Stage 1 is that teachers and practitioners use a systematic synthetic phonics approach to teach word recognition processes, and embed this within a language-rich curriculum to develop language knowledge and comprehension to facilitate reading comprehension. There is a national test for children at age six that aims to assess children's level of word recognition skill: the phonics screening check.

The phonics screening check

The phonics screening check is a test to see whether children have learned phonic sounds and can segment and blend them into words. It is taken by all year one children in a designated week in June. The test consists of 20 real words, such as *at, on, beg, sum*, and 20 pseudo words, such as *op, vap, osk, ect*. In the test, children are asked to read both the real and pseudo words, segmenting and blending them where necessary. Schools report the outcomes of the test to the local authority who then submit it to the Department for Education. Parents are given their child's score and told whether their child has met the standard by achieving a particular score.

The phonics screening test is not without controversy. At a practical level, many teachers argue that it is a time-consuming process that tells them no more than they already knew about children's abilities and needs (NFER, 2015). Additionally, teachers expressed some reservations about the phonics check for children who have English as an additional language (EAL) and children with special education needs. However, despite this, national data shows that children who have EAL achieved an almost identical level to children speaking English as their first language (DFE, 2014a). It is important to note that the phonics screening check is only assessing children's ability to decode text, so caution needs to be exercised in interpreting this data – as phonics has been shown to be necessary but not sufficient in reading acquisition, including for children who are bilingual.

There is an additional concern that it is inappropriate to have summative assessments that result in very young children being categorised and labelled so early in their school learning. For example, it is known that being a summer-born child can have a significant impact on learning in the early school years (Verachtert *et al.*, 2010; Rogers and Rose, 2007). At a more fundamental level, Professor Margaret Clark (2013) challenges the value and validity of the test. She argues that there are significant flaws in the test itself, in the process of administering the test, and what happens for the children who fail to meet the expected standard.

DEVELOP YOUR UNDERSTANDING

The phonics screening check

Professor Margaret Clark (2013, p3) lists the following concerns about the validity and value of the phonics screening test.

- No clear rationale has been provided for identifying 32 as meeting the expected standard.

- No clear explanation has been given for the inclusion of pseudo words in the test.

- No analysis has been undertaken of the contribution of the pseudo words to the final scores, yet more latitude is permitted in pronunciation of pseudo words than the real words.

- The evidence of a spike in the percentage of children gaining a mark of 32 rather than 31 in both years of administration of the test, a pass mark known to the teachers in advance raises serious questions about the validity of this test.

- The implications of a large difference in pass rate between the youngest and oldest children needs to be considered.

- The needs of those who failed to reach the arbitrary pass mark on this test may not be met by a focus on synthetic phonics as the solution to their problems.

Read her paper at **http://tactyc.org.uk/pdfs/Margaret%20Clark.pdf** and make sure that you understand these concerns about the test.

What is your view? Do you think that the check is useful? Is it valid? Give reasons for your view.

Rose and the pedagogy of phonics

In addition to providing a framework for understanding reading and defining the approach that should be used, Rose (2006) also draws some broad conclusions about the pedagogy of phonics teaching and developing comprehension. The review (2006) states that while both phonics and language comprehension should be taught, there will be shifts in the balance of focus as children become more fluent readers. Learning phonics and enabling children to read fluently is likely to be a time-limited task, while understanding and responding to texts in increasingly sophisticated ways is a process that will go on through schooling and beyond. Language comprehension, Rose (2006) concludes, can be developed through discourse and a wide range of good fiction and non-fiction, discussing characters, story content and interesting events. Word reading, in contrast, is likely to be as a result of direct instruction.

Rose's (2006) conclusion about the teaching of phonics has informed the way in which schools teach and test children's reading, and is evident in government guidance that defines the key features of an effective systematic synthetic phonics teaching programme (DFE, 2010a). Among other criteria, the schemes must

- present high-quality systematic, synthetic phonic work as the prime approach to decoding print, i.e. a phonics 'first and fast' approach;
- enable children to start learning phonic knowledge and skills using a systematic, synthetic programme by the age of five, with the expectation that they will be fluent readers having secured word recognition skills by the end of Key Stage 1;
- be designed for the teaching of discrete, daily sessions progressing from simple to more complex phonic knowledge and skills, and covering the major grapheme/phoneme correspondences.

Children learning English as an additional language (EAL)
The Simple View of Reading shows us that phonics is necessary but not sufficient to learn to read (and spell) effectively. In addition to phonics, children who are learning to read need to be able to comprehend what they are reading. Therefore, children who have English as an additional language similarly need to develop both their phonic ability, and their knowledge and understanding of English to enable them to comprehend the text.

The process of learning phonics is likely to be the same for children with EAL as for monolingual children.

- A strong focus on speaking and listening to enable children to tune into the English, to hear and pronounce sounds that make up the language.
- Phonemes, graphemes and their correspondence, segmenting and blending can all be taught in the same systematic way.
- Words that cannot be decoded – 'tricky words'– can also be taught and practised in the same way that they are taught to monolingual children.
- Pedagogically, children with EAL will benefit from active, visual, meaningfully contextualised activities and tasks. Again, this is the same as for monolingual children.

The other dimension of learning to read – comprehension – is more complex. Comprehension of text requires language knowledge to understand decoded words. This means that some children who are bilingual may be able to decode words effectively, having good phonic knowledge, but not understand what they have read as the words are outside their current vocabulary. Indeed, Burgoyne *et al.*'s (2011) study found exactly this – that children learning EAL often demonstrate fast and accurate reading accuracy skills, but lower levels of vocabulary knowledge place significant constraints on EAL learners' comprehension of spoken and written texts.

This demonstrates the importance of a rich language environment, with significant opportunities for children who have EAL to develop strong oral language, in both their home language (or languages) and in English, to support their language comprehension.

Phonics in the early years: tensions and debates

Despite the seemingly cohesive approach to teaching reading, there are significant concerns and debates about the appropriateness of this approach for very young children. As Rinaldi argues (Moss and Petrie, 2002), childhood and children's experiences of childhood do not just exist – we create them through ethical and political choices made within a wider framework of ideas and values. Concerns about the current approach to young children's learning, including early literacy, and the current framework of ideas, values and understandings that underpin this approach, are wide-ranging and focus on some fundamental aspects of education:

- what it means to become literate;
- what we know and understand about young children's learning;
- the validity of particular approaches to teaching and learning for our youngest children;
- the relationship between early years and later schooling.

What does it mean to become literate?

The current approach to teaching reading embeds a particular view of what it means to become literate and the reasons why we need to become literate. It is argued (Moss and Petrie, 2002; Moss, 2014) that central to this current approach is *education for employment*. The focus of schools, including becoming literate, is to prepare children for employment in an increasingly competitive world. Indeed, one of the current government's stated aims for early years is *helping to improve children's outcomes, and so putting them on the path to success in later life* (Ofsted, 2014).

School is, therefore, seen as preparation for a future that requires an educated, compliant and resourceful workforce (Moss and Petrie, 2002). Ball (2007) comments that *education is increasingly, indeed perhaps almost exclusively, spoken of within policy in terms of economic value and its contribution to international market competitiveness* (Ball, 2007, pp185–6). The understanding of early learning in this conceptualisation is, therefore, limited to a child's readiness to engage in the formal curriculum. So, becoming literate is viewed instrumentally: a vital skill for children to acquire in preparation for school-based learning and later employment, and development is viewed as a process induced by adults through planned focused activities, experiences and teaching. This current conceptualisation of what it means to become literate, and the place of school and literacy in children's lives is contested, with many arguing that becoming and being literate has far greater meaning in our lives than the current instrumental focus of school-based literacy.

Barton *et al.* (2000) argue that becoming literate is first and foremost a social practice, in that it is purposeful and meaningfully embedded in children's lives before and beyond school.

Literacy learning does not begin at school (Clay, 1991; Goouch and Lambrith, 2011; Flewitt, 2014). In their lives before and beyond school, children encounter many different kinds of literacies and gain a wealth of knowledge about literacy materials and practices (Flewitt, 2014). Therefore, children begin school rich in literacy experiences, for example:

- spoken language;
- awareness of environmental print such as supermarket names, logos and brands, menus and road signs;
- engagement with advertisements;
- use of technology for games and communication;
- reading fiction and non-fiction books;
- experience with drawing and art materials;
- observation of others' handwriting and using technology for writing for a range of purposes.

These experiences give literacy practices function and meaning for children, and enable them to engage with and shape experiences within their homes and communities: being literate is about making meaning within their lives, families and communities. What it means to become literate, therefore, has a wide and diverse meaning and focus. This understanding of literacy as social practice (Barton and Hamilton, 2000) has limited resonances with the current narrow skills-based focus in school.

DEVELOP YOUR UNDERSTANDING

Barton and Hamilton (2000) argue that literacy is a social practice and outline the six propositions below as the basis of their theory. Read their chapter *A social theory of literacy practices and events* to develop your understanding of this theory.

- Literacy is best understood as a set of social practices; these can be inferred from events which are mediated by written texts.
- There are different literacies associated with different domains of life.

(Continued)

- Literacy practices are patterned by social institutions and power relationships and some literacies are more dominant, visible and influential than others.

- Literacy practices are purposeful and embedded in broader social goals and cultural practices.

- Literacy is historically situated.

- Literacy practices change and new ones are frequently acquired through processes of informal learning and sense making.

Chapter available at: **http://e503.weebly.com/uploads/8/6/2/3/8623935/situated_literacies_-_ch._1.pdf**

The disparity between school-based understandings of what it means to become literate and literacy as social practice is reflected in Flewitt's (2010) study on multimodal literacies in the early years. The study examined what learning to be literate means for young children in today's media-rich world, and found significant differences between literacy experiences in settings and those beyond school.

They observed that in the current Foundation Stage curriculum, literacy is presented as an essentially solitary, print-based, linguistic accomplishment and, while there is clear guidance regarding the development of traditional literacy skills, scant attention is paid to new technologies and the implications of their ubiquitous use in everyday literacy practices.

This understanding of literacy was reflected in settings in the *corresponding emphasis on the linear acquisition of traditional literacy skills* (Flewitt, 2010, p2). In contrast to this, children's experiences at home involved engagement in a range of literacy experiences across diverse media: phones, TV, computers and 'smart' toys. The study concluded that becoming literate in today's world involves *mastery of diverse practices and technical skills, along with the ability to adapt, improvise, and identify relevant features in static and dynamic texts and to navigate around them* (Flewitt, 2010, p4).

One of the most vocal opponents of the current school-based understanding of what it means to become literate is the children's poet Michael Rosen. In his blog, his talks and at readings, Rosen (2013) argues passionately for the importance of reading for meaning and pleasure, and contends that the current approach to teaching reading through phonics 'first, fast and only' undermines the delight in books and reading. Drawing on his own reading of the debates and discussions with academics, he cites a range of reasons why reading is a process of making meaning as well as making the 'right noises'. He argues for a holistic view of reading in which meaning and enjoyment are as prized as the ability to decode words.

In addition, Rosen argues cogently against the phonics (and grammar) testing regimes in schools. Not only, he argues, do these tests make presumptions about the regularity of our language and the stability and usage of grammar, but they reduce the richness of language and expression to a series of skills to be learned, applied, tested and assessed as right or wrong. They also carry with them the potential to label young children as failures and turn them away from books and reading at a young age. Rosen's views were poetically expressed in a recent reading (n.d.).

'Come in,' said a woman in a loud voice.

Alice walked in to a large room at the Compartment of Edification.

Sitting in front of her, staring into the middle distance was the Blue Queen.

'How old are you?' said the Blue Queen.

'I'm seven years old,' said Alice politely.

Sitting next to the Queen was the Gibblet.

'Seven?' said the Gibblet. 'Seven? Test her.'

'Test her,' said the Blue Queen.

'Test me?' said Alice, 'but we've only just met.'

'And be robust,' said the Gibblet.

'And be robust,' said the Blue Queen.

Alice heard a scratching sound.

She looked round and observed a row of scribes scratching the word 'robust' on their scrolls.

'Why are you doing that?' enquired Alice.

'To tell the world the good news about robust tests,' they chorused.

'But how do you know 'Robust Tests' is good news?' asked Alice politely.

'Because the Blue Queen said it is,' chorused the scribes.

'Just because someone says something is something, doesn't mean that it is the thing they say it is,' said Alice.

'Test her!' shouted the Gibblet.

'Test her!' shouted the Blue Queen.

'Robustly,' said the Gibblet.

'Robustly,' said the Blue Queen.

'Why do you keep repeating what he says?' said Alice.

(Continued)

(Continued)

'How else would I know what to say?' said the Blue Queen.

'You could think for yourself,' said Alice.

'No, no, no!' screamed the Gibblet. 'That's why we have the tests.'

'What? To help people think for themselves?'

'No, the opposite, you little ninny,' screamed the Gibblet.

'I like opposites,' said Alice. 'I like thinking of things that don't have opposites, like a cupboard, or a coal scuttle.'

'You go on like that, you'll fail the test,' laughed the Gibblet.

'You go on like that, you'll fail the test,' laughed the Blue Queen.

'As far as I'm concerned you've both failed,' said Alice.

She turned round and walked out.

Rosen argues that we should create book-loving schools, where children have access to libraries, book clubs, magazines, books that tie in with films and TV shows, visits from authors and illustrators, visits to places of interest linked to and accompanied by books and stories, whole school projects based on books, the space and time to develop and express open-ended views about books, teachers who are readers and relish books, and compulsory joining in with a read-aloud session to close every teachers' meeting.

Similarly to Rosen, Davis (2012) in the paper outlined below argues from a philosophical point of view that the current approach to teaching reading challenges the very basis of what reading is: the rich, subtle process of interpreting and deriving meaning from text.

WHAT DOES RESEARCH TELL US?

A monstrous regime of synthetic phonics: fantasies of research based methods versus real teaching (Davis, 2012)

Davis's paper was originally given at the 2012 annual conference of The Philosophy of Education Society. In it he opposes the universal imposition of a very specific method of teaching reading that involves dealing with decoding text outside of the context of real reading contexts. He is clear that he is not attacking the employment of phonics as one way to teach young children to read, nor pronouncing on the claims of empirical evidence, but his aim is to challenge some of the conceptual and logical issues that underpin the current strong focus on the use of synthetic phonics to teach reading in the early years.

In his paper, Davis (2012) poses and responds to a series of issues.

(Continued)

First, he contends that the conceptual model apparently assumed by advocates of synthetic phonics and the 'simple view of reading' are conceptually flawed: decoding cannot be thought of independently of reading as there is a complex and interdependent relationship between phonemes, semantics and syntax; the reader's grasp of how constituents of spoken words blend to make whole words must encompass much more than types of physical sound. In developing his argument, Davis (2012) cites the following examples of heteronyms in which a reader would need to understand the meaning of the text before knowing how to pronounce it.

- I want to tear the book. She shed a tear.

- He is rowing with his wife. He is rowing with his wife.

- She only had a minute to put on her minute brooch before going out.

- The leading philosopher insulted the vicar. The leading on the church roof was damaged by the snowfall.

Second, Davis (2012) contends that someone delivering a rigidly prescribed synthetic phonics programme would not actually be teaching. He argues that empirical evidence, in particular randomised controlled trial (RCT) evidence, of the efficacy of teaching techniques is not analogous with RCT in other areas of research such as drug trials in medicine. This is because the set of activities categorised as intensive discrete phonics lessons, on which the evidence is based, are unlikely to possess the kind of common essence associated with RCT trials in other areas of research. Davis (2012) asks us to imagine ourselves in a real classroom where minute by minute teachers scan pupils' faces, behaviour and replies, seeking to diagnose levels of knowledge, understandings, concentration and motivation. Even over a short period of time, teachers use this information to make multitudes of decisions modifying their language, task focus, organisation and timing: subtle, sensitive pedagogical decision-making. This responsiveness to unpredictability *should*, he argues, be part of the lesson, indeed an essential part of professional behaviour. If students' responses were irrelevant, it would not be teaching because at the heart of teaching is the fundamental insight that a learner acquires new knowledge based on what they already know, and this requires constant monitoring and responsiveness by the teacher.

Finally, Davis (2012) contends that synthetic phonics has the potential to harm pupils who are beyond the beginning stage of reading. In line with his previous point, Davis (2012) asserts that state imposition of a teaching technique constitutes an approach that is delivered without being tempered by the cognitive and motivational states of the pupils. This, he argues, is justified on utilitarian grounds: that it benefits the majority of pupils so it is worth imposing on all pupils. This is the same with a number of other areas of learning included in the national curriculum: they are included as they are believed to benefit the majority of children and society as a whole. However, Davis (2012) contends that reading

(Continued)

should be regarded as a special case. He argues that reading is at the very heart of contemporary learning so is intimately bound up with an individual's ability to flourish. Children who arrive at school able to read, or well on their way to reading, should not, he argues, be subject to intensive phonics teaching. He believes that it is an affront to their emerging identities as persons, and potentially damaging, to reduce their engagement with the rich nourishing human activity of reading to a decontextualised skill. He acknowledges that this may be more complex pedagogically, meeting the actual needs of all the children in the group, but this highlights Davis's (2012) central opposition to the phonics question: the *universal* prescription of synthetic phonics.

Davis (2012) asserts that mechanical decoding wrenches children away from the rich and subtle process of interpreting and deriving meaning from text: efficiency in managing a class and a utilitarian approach to teaching reading should not take precedence over other human and educational values.

These views contest the current approach to early learning and challenge the notion that there is a single story about what it means to become literate, and the dominance of school and policy makers' views of what it means to become and to be literate. There is concern about the view of learning that embeds an understanding of the child as a passive recipient of knowledge skills and values, growing into a predetermined identity. Indeed, Eddington *et al.* (2011) argue that there is a strong conflict between the stated principle of the Early Years Foundation Stage (EYFS) that every child is a Unique Child and the EYFS learning goals that create an outcome-driven, skills-focused approach. This approach, they argue, challenges what we know about how young children learn and undermines pedagogical knowledge that informs *our delicate, subtle work with young children* (ibid., p40).

Young children learning

Young children learn and develop through being active in the world around them. They explore, investigate, observe and experience their world through all their senses, including through listening and engagement in talk. Talk and listening also enable children to develop language that gives them a powerful tool for understanding, thinking and communicating. Additionally, children learn best in a context of warm, secure and safe relationships (Bingham and Whitebread, 2012).

This need for active, exploratory, experiential, interactive learning is best met through play as it is widely acknowledged that play is a vital medium for young children's learning (Moyles, 2010; Broadhead *et al.*, 2010). This is recognised in the Early Years Foundation Stage (DFE, 2014), which states that *play is essential for children's development and that each area of learning and development must be implemented through planned purposeful play*. Play allows young children to learn actively. It is enjoyable, engaging and motivating, interactive and experiential. It allows children to explore and consolidate their current learning and provides challenge to move children's learning forward. Play cannot be wrong; it enables children to explore and investigate their world in a safe and secure way. It provides the opportunity for children to transform their knowledge and understanding through active, direct experience in their world, and to engage in concrete experiences that support the early stages of symbolic representation and later abstract thought. The earliest stages of becoming literate are similarly supported through active, meaningful experiences with literacy practices in the home and community.

Our understanding of how young children learn and develop is underpinned by developmental theory. There are a number of influential theorists, pioneers and thinkers in early years whose work articulates why an active, play-based, exploratory and interactive learning environment, in the context of warm, supportive relationships, will best support the learning and development needs of young children – for example, Piaget, Vygotsky, Bowlby and Bronfenbrenner's theories, the ideas of Froebel, Macmillan and Isaacs, and the pedagogical approaches of Steiner and Montessori (Gray and MacBlain, 2015).

There are, therefore, significant tensions between the demands for greater formal teaching at an increasingly earlier age, and the commitment within the EYFS of play-based learning that allows for active, experiential engagement with a wide range of activities and experiences. It is observable that current early years' policy that sees the purpose of early years as 'readying' children for later schooling, has resulted in some areas of the curriculum, such as literacy, becoming focused on the acquisition of predetermined knowledge and skills, and a subsequent increase in a teacher-led pedagogy.

Early years and later schooling

Historically, there has been a clear and accepted distinction between early years and school, which included distinctly different learning spaces, pedagogical practices, aims and outcomes. However, the recent political imperative to align early years with statutory schooling has challenged this distinction, resulting in a change in the relationship between early years and later schooling. Early years is now seen first and foremost as a preparation for later schooling, with an outcome-driven, prescribed curriculum, The Early Years Foundation Stage (EYFS) (DFE, 2014), which has changed the educational provision and experience for our youngest children. This is particularly notable in literacy where the current requirements in EYFS are that children begin the formal learning of phonics, with expectations that by the end of the Foundation Stage children will be proficient in their use of phonics for reading and writing. The Early Learning Goals (DFE, 2013, pp21–2) for reading and writing are as follows.

> *Children read and understand simple sentences. They use phonic knowledge to decode regular words and read them aloud accurately. They also read some common irregular words. They demonstrate understanding when talking with others about what they have read.*

> *Children use their phonic knowledge to write words in ways which match their spoken sounds. They also write some irregular common words. They write simple sentences which can be read by themselves and others. Some words are spelt correctly and others are phonetically plausible.*

This recent change of focus in early years, away from a fluid, child-centred approach towards an outcome-based curriculum is regarded by many in the field of early years as *Too Much, Too Soon?* (House, 2011) for many of our youngest children. The stronger emphasis on predetermined outcomes and the demand for more formal, teacher-led approaches to learning, particularly in phonics, have resulted in early years teaching and learning becoming increasingly like school-based learning, and this 'schoolifying' of the early childhood years goes against what we know about what enables young children to thrive. As Bingham and Whitebread (2012) argue, the evidence suggests overwhelmingly that children's development is enhanced in contexts where they experience emotional warmth and security, feelings of being in control of the events and activities in which they engage, where they experience appropriate levels of cognitive challenge and ample opportunities to speak and reflect about their own learning. In addition, children need playful contexts in which their learning is sensitively supported by adults.

These tensions and debates about developmentally appropriate provision in the early years have strong resonances with phonics teaching. There is significant concern that, in the absence of a good understanding of what comes before phonics, practitioners and teachers are starting direct and explicit teaching of phonics with our youngest children before they have the knowledge, understanding and skill to enable them to access this teaching with a good chance of success. It is, therefore, important that practitioners and teachers working with young children have a good understanding of what comes before phonics so that provision offers children the opportunity to develop a range of knowledge and skills. In addition, knowing what comes before phonics is necessary in order that effective assessments can be made about children's abilities so that explicit, direct phonics teaching only begins when children have a high chance of successfully engaging with the teaching.

What comes before phonics?

Imagine an iceberg. The tip of the iceberg peeps out from the water, supported beneath by a huge body of ice. This is a good analogy for learning to read. The tip represents the visible skills of reading and writing, which are supported by a huge body of knowledge, understandings, skills and attitudes that underpin it. The robustness and strength of the tip is supported and underpinned by what lies beneath.

Using this analogy, learning phonics is underpinned by a range of knowledge, understandings, skills and attitudes that are learned and developed in early childhood. This range of knowledge and skills increases the likelihood of young children coming to phonics teaching ready to learn and with a high chance of success. Knowledge and skills include:

- spoken language: the basis of becoming literate;
- physical activity that supports sensory awareness and integration;
- meta-linguistic awareness;

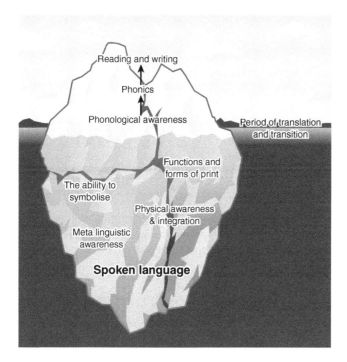

Figure 1.2   What comes before phonics

- an understanding of the functions and forms of print;
- the ability to symbolise;
- phonological awareness.

This knowledge, skills and understanding create a framework for what come before phonics. However, it is important to understand that becoming literate is a fluid and dynamic process, so this framework is not a prescribed set of outcomes. The framework brings together what is known about early experiences that enable children to become literate, including accessing phonics teaching successfully, and thus provides a basis for understanding, and providing for, early literacy in early years settings and schools.

Conclusion

This chapter has considered the current approach to teaching reading at Foundation Stage and Key Stage 1, in particular the strong emphasis on systematic synthetic phonics. It has highlighted the implications of this for children who are learning English as an additional language. The chapter has outlined what we understand about how very young children learn, and discussed different views on what it means to become literate. It has examined the relationship between early learning and later school, and highlighted the tensions in the 'schoolification' of early years. The chapter emphasises the importance of professional knowledge about the teaching of reading, including what comes before formal teaching of phonics, so that as teachers and practitioners we are able to make developmentally appropriate provision for children.

References

Ball, S (2007) *Education PLC: Understanding Private Sector Participation in Public Sector Education*. London: Routledge.

Barton, D, Hamilton, M and Ivanic, R (2000) *Situated Literacies: Reading and Writing in Context*. London: Routledge.

Bingham, S and Whitebread, D (2012) School readiness: A critical review of perspectives and evidence. A TACTYC publication. Now available as: Whitebread, D and Bingham, S (2011) *School readiness: A critical review of perspectives and evidence*. Available online at: **http://tactyc.org.uk/occasional-papers/** (accessed July 2015, but no results found 11 September 2016).

Bowlby, J (1953) *Child Care and the Growth of Love*. London: Penguin.

Broadhead, P, Howard, J and Wood, E (eds) (2010) *Play and Learning in the Early Years*. London: SAGE.

Broberg, AG (2000) A review of interventions in the parent–child relationship informed by attachment theory. *Acta Paediatrica*, 89: 37–42.

Burgoyne, K, Whiteley, HE and Hutchinson, JM (2011) The development of comprehension and reading-related skills in children learning English as an additional language and their monolingual, English-speaking peers. *British Journal of Educational Psychology*, 81(2): 344–54.

Clark, M (2013) The phonics check for Year 1 children in England: Unresolved issues of its value and validity after two years. Available online at: **http://tactyc.org.uk/pdfs/Margaret%20Clark.pdf** (accessed 11 September 2016).

Clay, M (1991) *Becoming Literate: The Construction of Inner Control*. London: Heinemann.

Davis, A (2012) A monstrous regime of synthetic phonics: Fantasies of research based methods versus real teaching. *Journal of Philosophy of Education*, 46(4): 560–73.

DFE (2010) The importance of teaching. Available online at: **www.gov.uk/government/uploads/system/uploads/attachment_data/file/175429/CM-7980.pdf** (accessed 11 September 2016).

DFE (2010a) Phonics teaching materials: Core criteria and the self-assessment process. Available online at: **www.gov.uk/government/uploads/system/uploads/attachment_data/file/298420/phonics_core_criteria_and_the_self-assessment_process.pdf** (accessed 11 September 2016).

DFE (2011) Teachers' Standards. Available online at: **www.gov.uk/government/uploads/system/uploads/attachment_data/file/283566/Teachers_standard_information.pdf** (accessed 11 September 2016).

DFE (2013) Early years outcomes. Available online at: **www.foundationyears.org.uk/files/2012/03/Early_Years_Outcomes.pdf** (accessed 11 September 2016.

DFE (2014) Statutory framework for the early years. Available online at: **www.gov.uk/government/uploads/system/uploads/attachment_data/file/335504/EYFS_framework_from_1_September_2014__with_clarification_note.pdf** (accessed 11 September 2016).

DFE (2014a) Phonics screening check and key stage 1 assessments. Available online at: **www.gov.uk/government/statistics/phonics-screening-check-and-key-stage-1-assessments-england-2014** (accessed 11 September 2016).

DFE/NCTL (2013) Teachers' Standards (early years). Available online at: **www.gov.uk/government/uploads/system/uploads/attachment_data/file/211646/Early_Years_Teachers__Standards.pdf** (accessed 11 September 2016).

Eddington, M, House, R, Oldfield, L and Palmer, S (2011) Challenging Government Policy Making for the Early Years. In House, R (2011) (ed.) *Too Much, Too Soon? Early Learning and the Erosion of Childhood*. Stroud: Hawthorne Press.

Ellis, S and Moss, G (2013) Ethics, education policy and research: The phonics question reconsidered. Available online at: **http://clie. org.uk/wpcontent/uploads/2013/10/Ellis_Moss_2013.pdf** (accessed October 2016).

Flewitt, R (2010) Multimodal literacies in the early years. CREET: The Open University. Available online at: **www.open.ac.uk/creet/ main/sites/www.open.ac.uk.creet.main/files/04%20Multimodal%20Literacy.pdf** (accessed 11 September 2016).

Flewitt, R (2014) Early Literacy Learning in the Contemporary Age. In Moyles, J, Georgeson, J and Payler, J (eds) (2014). *Early Years Foundations: Critical Issues* (2nd edn). Berkshire: Oxford University Press.

Goouch, C and Lambrith, A (2011) *Teaching Early Reading and Phonics*. London: SAGE.

Gray, C and MacBlain, S (2015) *Learning Theories in Childhood*. London: SAGE.

House, R (ed.) (2011) *Too Much, Too Soon? Early Learning and the Erosion of Childhood*. Stroud: Hawthorne Press.

Johnston, R and Watson, J (2005) The effects of synthetic phonics teaching on reading and spelling attainment: A seven year longitudinal study. Available online at: **www.gov.scot/Resource/Doc/36496/0023582.pdf** (accessed 11 September 2016).

Moss, P (2014) *Transformative Change and Real Utopias in Early Childhood Education: A Story of Democracy, Experimentation and Potentiality*. London: Routledge.

Moss, P and Petrie, P (2002) *From Children's Services to Children's Spaces*. London: RoutledgeFalmer.

Moyles, J (2010) *The Excellence of Play* (3rd edn). Berkshire: Oxford University Press.

NFER (2015) Phonics screening check evaluation: Final report. Available online at: **www.gov.uk/government/uploads/system/ uploads/attachment_data/file/434821/RR418A_Phonics_screening_check_evaluation.pdf** (accessed 11 September 2016).

Ofsted (2014) The Report of Her Majesty's Chief Inspector of Education, Children's Services and Skills. Early Years. Available online at: **www. ofsted.gov.uk/earlyyearsannualreport1213** (accessed October 2016).

Phonics International (2012) The Simple View of Reading and The Simple View of Writing models. Available online at: **www. phonicsinternational.com/The_Simple_View_of_Reading_model.pdf** (accessed 11 September 2016).

Rogers, S and Rose, J (2007) Ready for Reception? The advantages and disadvantages of single point entry to school. *Early Years*, 27(1): 47–63.

Rose, J (2006) Independent review of the teaching of early reading. Available online at: **http://dera.ioe.ac.uk/5551/2/report.pdf** (accessed 11 September 2016).

Rosen, M (no date) A book-loving school. Available online at: **www.michaelrosen.co.uk/booklovingschool.html** (accessed 11 September 2016).

Rosen, M (2013) Phonics: A summary of my views. Available online at: **http://michaelrosenblog.blogspot.co.uk/2013/01/ phonics-summary-of-my-views.html** (accessed 11 September 2016).

TDA (2011) Systematic synthetic phonics in initial teaching training: Guidance and support materials. 2011 notes issued to ITT providers by TDA. London: DFE.

Verachtert, P, De Fraine, B, Onghena, P and Ghesquière, P (2010) Season of birth and school success in the early years of primary education. *Oxford Review of Education*, 36(3): 285–306.

2   Leading into literacy

Introduction

Becoming literate starts in a child's very youngest years in the everyday uses of literacy in their family and community. Authentic engagement with print, for example, recognising the sign of a familiar supermarket, observing adults messaging, and 'reading' the print on clothing and toys begins children's journey to becoming a reader and a writer.

This chapter explores the early experiences and interactions that facilitate later literacy learning. Research shows that there are particular experiences in early life, at home and in pre-school settings that lead into literacy – experiences that enable children to access literacy teaching with purpose, enjoyment and with a high chance of success. The chapter focuses on the broader context of early literacy knowledge and skills in anticipation of the narrower focus on what comes before phonics in later chapters. It looks at what leads into literacy at home and in settings, and the role of adults in facilitating these experiences and interactions. It considers provision in the learning environment in pre-school settings and reflects critically on some of the assumptions that we make about children's engagement with activities and experiences in settings.

Early experiences and interactions at home that facilitate literacy learning

Think about all the ways in which you engage with literacy in your day-to-day life. Perhaps as you wake up you reach for your phone, and read and write posts and messages. The food that you eat will have packaging and dates that you read. As you drive or catch a bus, you will engage with a wealth of written signs and directions and instructions. You may browse the Internet or social media, scrolling between pages and posts, moving across up and down text and images. In shops you will be assailed by labels, advertising, offers, directions, signs and instructions which you will read to help you make choices about what you buy. Your clothing and footwear, bags and accessories are likely to have logos and print on them. In addition to reading and writing, you will talk to people as you move through the day, changing the tone and register of your interaction depending on who you are talking to, and the purpose of the interaction. You will use language in a wide range of ways – to meet your needs, to manage others, to interact, to elicit information, to express views and ideas, to imagine and to communicate knowledge. Children grow up in this literate environment, surrounded by talking, reading and writing that has purpose and meaning. They observe and are involved in these and other everyday uses of language and literacy. In addition to these everyday experiences, most children will also have toys and books, games and technology that enable them to experience print in purposeful, meaningful and enjoyable ways. It is these experiences, in children's homes and communities that lead into later literacy learning in settings and schools.

Emergent literacy

This process of children's engagement with talking, reading and writing in their everyday lives is called 'emergent literacy'. Emergent literacy refers to knowledge and skills that children acquire prior to formal literacy learning (Edwards, 2014). It includes children's oral language ability, and their developing awareness and knowledge about the purposes and functions of reading and writing. More specifically, it includes concepts such as knowledge of print (left-to-right, top-to-bottom tracking) concepts about books (pictures/print, cover, page turning), and alphabet knowledge and good visual processing skills, all of which have been shown to be predictors of later literacy achievement (NELP, 2008). Dooley and Matthews (2009) extend this understanding to include emergent comprehension, which refers to the unfolding of children's understanding of their first tangible world of people, places and objects as well as the intangible, values, norms and learning processes; it is a child's active engagement in making meaning from play, daily routines, interaction and print (p291). Children's exploration of print in their environment and everyday lives enables them to build concepts about reading and writing – what it is, how it works and what it is used for, and supports the process of comprehension. These concepts are assimilated and accommodated (Gray and MacBlain, 2015) through multiple interactions and experiences, becoming more complex and differentiated with time and experience (Dooley and Mathews, 2009).

The research focus below identifies the ways in which families provide for and engage children in emergent literacy practices. Shea (2011) refers to these interactions in the home as *soft teaching*, in which parents encourage, respond, coach and answer questions, and children watch, reflect and ask as their curiosity is sparked by the behaviours of others, and replicate observed reading and writing behaviours in their play and interactions.

WHAT DOES RESEARCH TELL US?

Maternal literacy practices and toddlers' emergent literacy skill (Edwards, 2014)

Edwards's aims in this research (2014) was to examine home literacy environments to gain a better understanding of early literacy practices in the home.

The study involved visiting 15 mothers and their child at home, to assess observe and discuss shared reading activities and the home literacy environment. All the mothers were

(Continued)

from middle to upper socio-economic backgrounds with a mean age of 35.2 years and a mean education level of 19 years. There were 8 boys and 7 girl children with a mean age of 26.73 months. All the children were from full-term, non-eventful pregnancies, and there were no parental concerns about hearing, vision or communication.

The first visit involved assessment of the child's level of development using standardised tests and observation of both the child and the home environment. During the second visit Edwards videotaped the mother and child reading together. In the final visit she observed another shared reading activity and the parents answered a questionnaire on the home literacy environment and their beliefs and practices. During the shared reading sessions parents were asked to read particular books which included ABC books, rhyming books and novel books (p60).

From this study, Edwards (2014) drew a series of conclusions about the impact of the home learning environment and mother–child interactions on children's emergent literacy.

Home literacy environment

- The home environments were rich in print-related artefacts. This included environmental print including works of art with print/text, books, magazines, children's books, computer, lists, notes, calendars and literacy-focused toys. The mothers viewed literacy as both necessary and pleasurable, and literacy-based activities were an important part of their daily lives – for example, using the computer to access the Internet.

Emergent literacy behaviours of mothers and toddlers

Mothers

- The mothers engaged in emergent literacy behaviours associated with the written domain – for example, pointing to the text, turning pages, talking about the characters.
- Phonological awareness behaviours – for example, rhyming – were not observed.
- The mothers structured their days to provide literacy-rich experiences for the children – for example, story-book reading each day.

Toddlers

- The toddlers displayed observable emergent literacy skills consistent with the written language domain. Book conventions and story grammar were the most frequently observed occurrences of emergent literacy. Some behaviours associated with letter knowledge were also observed.
- The toddlers did not exhibit behaviours associate with print conventions.

Edwards (2014) concludes that the way in which the mothers interact with the children may facilitate emergent literacy behaviours and that the interaction begins the process

(Continued)

WHAT DOES RESEARCH TELL US? *continued*

of moving towards literacy. She notes that the mother's focus in the interactions is commensurate with early and later development of literacy skills and knowledge. She argues that this confirms Purcell Gates's (1994, 1996, 2001) model of emergent literacy behaviours: that children's emergent literacy has a written to oral progression, from knowledge about print conventions to phonological and letter awareness.

DEVELOP YOUR UNDERSTANDING

Edwards's (2014) study was undertaken with mothers from middle and high socio-economic status groups. In her conclusions she recognises that this is a limitation in generalising her findings to other groups.

- What is the relationship between socio-economic status and learning to read?

- What are the reasons given for this?

- Find out about ways in which we are trying to address this issue.

Edwards's (2014) research confirms what is clearly documented by research, that homes where talk and literacy practices are embedded in family and community enable children to move into literacy with ease. Melhuish *et al.* (2008, p. 106) concluded similarly that the home literacy environment is highly significant, and noted that:

> *While other family factors such as parents' education and SES* socio-economic status *are also important, the extent of home learning activities exerts a greater and independent influence on educational attainment.*

All children will come to pre-school settings and school with some knowledge of literacy acquired at home. However, as we have seen, this will vary depending on the child's family and community: some children's experiences will enable them to come to settings and school with a wealth of literacy knowledge and a range of skills that enable them to access teaching and learning with ease. Other children's experiences in their families and communities will be more limited in terms of how they enable children to access learning in settings and schools. This is important, because setting and school-based learning requires particular knowledge and skills which some families and communities enable children to develop, while literacy practices within other families and communities serve the needs of the community but don't necessarily enable the children to access setting and school-based learning. Marsh's (2003) research, outlined in detail below, is a good example of this. She found that some children's home literacy practices were strongly focused on media and popular culture, while school literacy practices were *a celebration of literacy practices which are entrenched in the socio-cultural lives of middle class groups* (Marsh, 2003, p370). Her study highlights the ways in which literacy practices in some families and communities are able to prepare children for learning in settings and schools, while for some children there is a dissonance between their experiences at home, and the expectations and practices in schools and settings.

WHAT DOES RESEARCH TELL US?

One-way traffic? Connections between literacy practice at home and in the nursery (Marsh, 2003)

Marsh's (2003) study looked at the literacy practices of a group of three- and four-year-old children. The children attended a nursery in a city in the North of England. The nursery served a predominantly white and working-class community. The community lived primarily in council housing and there was a high level of unemployment in the area.

Eighteen families completed a four-week literacy diary which documented all the texts read and written by the children. The diaries asked for parents and carers to document a wide range of texts: television and film; computer games; comics, books and environmental print. In addition, fifteen parents were interviewed to explore the home literacy practices in more detail.

Once the diaries had been analysed, the head teacher was asked to indicate which of the children's home literacy practices were commonly reflected in the nursery curriculum.

A number of findings came from the study.

- In the domain of the child's bedroom, or space in the living area that they used, many of the texts related to popular culture and televisual texts. These texts permeated the children's encounters with literacy.

- In the wider domain of the home, children encountered texts used and created in everyday life: environmental print, greetings cards, the Bible.

- While there were some similarities between the literacy practices at nursery and the wider domain of the home, there were fewer similarities between the child's domain and nursery. For example, although children encountered books at home and at nursery, the books they read at home and the books they read at nursery were very different for the children in this study. In the main, the books the children read at home were related to popular television programmes, retellings of Disney fairy stories, alphabet books and non-fiction texts. Most were purchased at supermarkets and other non-specialist shops. Very few of the books were the ones that can be found in nursery schools, books that comprise the early years 'canon' of well-loved texts.

(Continued)

- The early literacy curriculum, as perceived by the head of the nursery school, did not reflect the rich range of these children's home literacy experiences, even though the staff were sensitive to the need to ensure that media practices were included in their planning.

- Many of the parents interviewed were unable to provide examples of the ways in which home literacy practices have impacted upon the nursery, but were able to provide instances of activities that were brought from the nursery into the home.

Marsh (2003) concluded that the existing theories of literacy in the early years place undue emphasis on particular books, traditional forms of print literacy, individualised writing practices and literacy-related play experiences based on middle-class norms, and that these need to be challenged if the literacy traffic is to flow in both directions for children and families from all cultural and socio-economic groups.

DEVELOP YOUR UNDERSTANDING

What is your view about the use of popular culture in schools and settings?

- What are the advantages of this for the children?

- What are the disadvantages for the children?

- Consider the advantages and disadvantages in terms of literacy development.

- What criteria would you use for selecting which popular culture characters or stories to use?

What is clear is that these earliest experiences of talking, listening and engagement with literacy practices in the home and community shape children's early learning, and develop a range of knowledge, understanding, skills, and attitudes that can lead into later literacy learning. The relationship between these early experiences and later learning is well observed, and the subject of significant research activity and evidence. There is now growing interest and focus in neuroscience on how children's earliest experiences in their families and communities impact on later learning and development. Harvard University Center on the Developing Child argues that these earliest experiences are vital in shaping brain architecture, which is the foundation of all later learning and development. In accordance with what we observe about rich early language experiences having a positive impact on later learning, they conclude that science now shows us that having responsive relationships with adults, growth-promoting experiences, and healthy environments helps young children to build sturdy brain architecture.

35

Brain architecture (Harvard University's Center on the Developing Child, ND)

Harvard University's Center on the Developing Child was founded in 2006 with the aim of understanding and supporting the learning capacity, health, and economic and social mobility of young children, through science-based research and development.

Their work focuses on the impact of brain development on learning, behaviour and health. Their research concludes that early experiences affect the development of brain architecture, which provides the foundation for all later learning, behaviour and mental health. Adverse experiences in early life, they conclude, can impair brain architecture and this has negative effects into adulthood.

The developing brain

Brains are built over time from the bottom up. The basic brain architecture is constructed through an on-going process that begins before birth and continues into adulthood. Simple neural connections are made first, then more complex circuits. In the first few years of life 700–1,000 new neural connections are made every second. After this period of rapid growth, connections are reduced by a process called 'pruning' to enable brain circuits to become more efficient.

Brain architecture consists of billions of connections between individual neurons across different areas of the brain. The early years are the most active period for establishing these connections. The connections that form early provide the foundation for connections that are formed later.

The developing brain is shaped by the interactions of genes and experiences. Genes and experiences work together to shape the developing brain. Genes provide the blueprint for the formation of brain circuits, then the interaction between children and their parents, caregivers, family and community shapes brain development. Where this interaction and care is absent or inappropriate, the brain's architecture does not develop as expected, which can lead to issues with learning and behaviour.

Cognitive, emotional and social capacities are inextricably linked. The brain is highly integrated, so these capacities work in coordination with one another. Emotional well-being and social competence provide a strong foundation for emerging cognitive abilities. Therefore, emotional and social capacity, physical health and the cognitive and linguistic abilities that emerge in the early years are vital as a foundation for success at school and in later life.

Toxic stress weakens the architecture of the developing brain. The stress response activates a wide range of physiological reactions that are designed to prepare the body to deal with threat. If these responses stay activated at high levels for significant periods of time without supportive relationships to calm them, the child experiences 'toxic stress'.

(Continued)

WHAT DOES RESEARCH TELL US? continued

This toxic stress can impair the development of neural connections, especially in the area of the brain dedicated to higher order skills.

The central message about brain architecture is that it is easier, and ultimately less costly to the individual and to society, to form strong brain circuits during the early years than it is to intervene or try and fix things later.

DEVELOP YOUR UNDERSTANDING

Questioning neuroscience

Wastell and White (2012) challenge the discourse that has emerged around neuroscience and early years. They argue that the belief that a child's first three years are critical created a *now-or-never imperative to intervene before irreparable damage is done to the infant brain*. They contend that the infant brain is not readily susceptible to permanent and irreversible damage, rather, *plasticity and resilience seem to be the general rule* (Wastell and White, 2012, p. 397), and that the co-option of neuroscience has silenced vital moral debate, pushing practice in the direction of standardised, targeted interventions rather than simpler forms of family and community support.

- Find out more about the uses of neuroscience to explain children's learning.

- What are the benefits of using neuroscience to understand children's learnings and development?

- What are the limitations of this approach to understanding children's learnings and development?

- As a practitioner, how may findings from neuroscience inform and/or restrict your professional role?

Early years provision that supports literacy learning

The role of early years provision in supporting and developing children's early literacy learning is underpinned by the same principles as early literacy experiences in the home: children need a rich literacy environment with many opportunities for talking and listening, and engagement in literacy practices that are developmentally appropriate, purposeful and meaningful. This involves creating a literate environment in the setting, so that children are surrounded by print and engage with it in their environment and in the routines in the day. It also involves actively providing opportunities for the children to use emergent reading and writing in their play. These opportunities need to be meaningful within the context of the play activity. The case study below is an example of how nursery staff supported and developed children's play to involve literacy practices. In this way, the children were drawn into literacy practices in their play which enabled them to come to know about the forms and functions of print, and actively engage in meaning making in their play – both significant aspects of what comes before phonics (*see* Chapter 6).

CASE STUDY

Developing emergent reading and writing in child-initiated play

The boys in the nursery loved playing at police. They created and played out elaborate narratives all ending with the police chasing 'baddies', arresting them, and taking them down to the police station. The staff had provided dressing-up clothes and equipment and, with the children's help, created a police station and cells. This included opportunities for reading and writing through labels, signs, directions, name badges, posters, paper and pens, and a computer. The boys enjoyed this so the staff enhanced their play by joining in and introducing different ideas. On one day the staff joined in and introduced some specific vocabulary, such as suspect, charge, interview and crime scene. On another day they joined in and introduced the idea of using digital cameras and the computer to take pictures of the crime scene and suspects, and to label them. On another day they joined in and introduced the idea of using police notebooks to record what happened at the crime scene, and what the suspects said when interviewed at the police station.

The 'Matthew effect' of early literacy experiences

These early experiences with talking and listening, books, print and technology are vital as children move into becoming readers and writers. The significance of this is supported by the substantial and long-term evidence of the benefits to children's learning when talk and literacy are embedded in family and community life. Conversely, there is substantial evidence that when children don't have these early experiences becoming literate is more difficult (*see* Adams, 1990; Clay, 1991; Hartas, 2011). Stanovich (1986) terms this the 'Matthew effect'. The 'Matthew effect' references the biblical verse Matthew 25:29, The Parable of the Talents:

> *For unto every one that hath shall be given, and he shall have abundance: but from him that hath not shall be taken away even that which he hath.*

Stanovich uses this as an analogy for becoming literate: the rich get richer and the poor get poorer. He observes that there are accumulated advantages for children whose early experiences are rich in talking and listening, and engagement with print. These children tend to move into becoming readers and writers with relative ease and find literacy engaging and enjoyable. They thus remain involved and interested in literacy practices and so their literacy skills grow and improve – the rich get richer. In contrast, children whose early experiences don't involve sufficient engagement in activities that promote interest and enjoyment in literacy are more likely to find moving into becoming a reader and writer more difficult. Therefore, they are less likely to engage with literacy for enjoyment and with interest, and consequently less likely to develop fluent, effective literacy skills – the poor get poorer.

Provision in early childhood settings must therefore focus on rich literacy provision, with opportunities for children to engage in meaningful activities and experiences to support their emergent understandings about print and its place in our lives and learning. This needs to be evident in the continuous and enhanced provision, both indoors and outside, and in the routines and the setting's environment.

Continuous provision

This refers to the free-flow, child-initiated, play-based activities that are provided each day in a setting. In terms of provision for literacy, this needs to include opportunities for children to use their emerging literacy skills in purposeful ways. Activities and experiences need to embed opportunities for children to use their emerging reading and writing in meaningful ways – for example, the provision of menus, recipes, order lists, paper and pencils, maps, stickers, boxes and labels in an outdoor pizza-delivery role-play area.

Enhanced provision

This refers to the focused planned activities that are adult initiated. This includes specific planned activities that focus on early literacy, often in small groups. It can also refer to when an adult plays alongside children with an objective in mind and weaves the learning into the activity, using opportunities that arise to teach, consolidate or develop a skill or concept – for example, teaching about forms and functions of print by writing children's names on paintings whilst explaining why names are needed, pointing out that they are starting on the left and tracking right, and sounding out the child's name.

CASE STUDY

Enhanced provision for early literacy

The nursery teacher, Lisa, planned a table-top activity based around a farm set, in line with the nursery's topic on animals. As the children came to the activity Lisa asked them if they could help the farmer, and began with a story. The story told of how in the night the farmer had been woken by the sound of the wind whipping round the house, and the bellowing and baaing from the animals. He awoke to find that the fences had all been blown down and lots of the animals had escaped from their own fields into other fields. The task of sorting all the animals out and counting them was going to be a big task – could they help?

(Continued)

The children were then encouraged to sort out the animals and then, so the farmer was sure that no animals were lost, to count and record the number of animals. The children were given large sheets of paper and writing equipment, and recorded the information for the farmer.

This recording was supported by Lisa, who encouraged the children to make marks, draw and/or attempt to write words using phonics according to their abilities. She mediated the children's learning in a number of ways including:

- thanking the children for recording this for the farmer as now he had all the information that he needed to check that his animals were safe–indicating an important function of print;

- by articulating what they were doing – for example, 'I can see that there are three cows in the field and you have drawn 1–2–3 cows – making clear links between the activity and recording through mark making;

- by modelling writing, pointing out writing conventions, letter formation, and blending and segmenting words as she wrote observed by the children;

- by direct teaching of writing conventions – for example, ensuring that children who could make an attempt at writing words started at the left and tracked right, by articulating letter sounds (phonemes) as children wrote, and by modelling blending and segmenting words.

In this way the children were drawn into understanding aspects of the forms and functions of print in a way that was enjoyable, purposeful and meaningful.

The environment and routines

This refers to the overall learning environment, such as labels, instructions and displays, and the everyday routines in the setting, such as hanging up coats, registration and snack time. The setting needs to create a literate environment where children are surrounded by print, so that they come to know how and in what ways print is used and useful – for example, pictures and the accompanying world of wildlife that children may see in the outdoor area pinned on fences or hanging from trees; name cards for children to self-register or indicate when they have had a snack.

This provision provides for children's earliest engagement with talk and print, and is essential in ensuring that they enjoy books and become increasingly interested in using their emergent literacy knowledge and skills in their play. The 'Matthew effect' of this is that children become interested in books and print, and begin to recognise the means and uses of literacy, and the resulting knowledge and skills lead into later literacy learning. As Purcell Gates (1994, 1996, 2001 in Edwards, 2014) argues, children's emergent literacy has a written-to-oral progression: from knowledge about print conventions to phonological and letter awareness.

Ensuring inclusion in provision

All early years settings are required to meet the needs of all children. The activities and experiences provided need to be available for all children, so provision needs to be carefully considered and, when appropriate, adapted to enable this to happen. For example, there may be children in the setting who have English as an additional language or children with identified or emerging special educational needs, so provision will need to be adapted so that these children can engage in activities and experiences alongside their peers, in ways that are commensurate with their abilities and needs. There is a range of ways in which this can be achieved. In terms of specific activities and experiences that lead into literacy, these may include the following.

• Opportunities to actively engage in physical activity, to develop balance, coordination, proprioception, and develop sensory awareness and integration (*see* Chapter 4).

• Augmentative communication, such as staff using Makaton signs to support spoken language, communication aids and objects of reference.

• Visual and tactile signs and displays around the setting using photographs, pictures or Makaton symbols.

• Books provided in different formats; talking books, bilingual books.

• An appropriate sensory diet for the children, which may include activities to engage and stimulate children's senses in different ways and/or reduce sensory stimulation when needed.

• Opportunities for mark making provided indoors and out, large scale and small, on the floor, walls and boards, with a wide variety of large and small mark-making materials.

• Hardware and software that supports access to the technology through tactile, visual and auditory means.

• The use of technology to support access to activities, such as recorded instructions at activities for children to listen and respond to headsets to listen to stories.

It is worth noting that while these adaptations to activities and experiences may be put in place to support the needs of specific children, or groups of children, these adaptations will also benefit all the other children in the setting. For example, the use of augmentative communication (signs and symbols) will support all children's language acquisition and development, and enable all children to become increasingly independent, personally and in their learning; physical activity that supports sensory awareness and integration is vital for all children's later learning; and an interesting variety of mark-making activities and equipment, provided inside and outside, is likely to encourage all children to become involved in mark making.

Early literacy and socio-economic status

While provision for early literacy in settings is clearly important for all children, it is particularly vital for children who have not had these experiences beyond school: children who grow up in homes in which books, reading and other literacy practices are very limited. There is a wide body of evidence that recognises that there is a significant relationship between a child's family background and literacy achievement: we know that socio-economic status is strongly related to education outcomes (Basit *et al.*, 2015; Hartas, 2011; EEF, n.d.), and evidence from round the world shows that there is a high correlation between social disadvantage and poor literacy (Buckingham *et al.*, 2013). Therefore, as Stanovich's (1986) Matthew effect points out, unless these children are given opportunities when they are young to become interested in books and reading, and develop early literacy knowledge and skills, there is a high risk that their poor early start in literacy will result in ongoing poor literacy levels. The reasons for this are many, complex and multilayered, so while we can observe and document this relationship, we are yet to fully understand it. For example, Hartas (2011) concluded that

> *despite that most parents from diverse backgrounds invested frequently in home learning, children living in poverty and children of mothers without any educational qualifications fared less well in language / literacy and social development, compared to their peers in educationally and economically well-off families.*

(Hartas, 2011, pp11–12)

Interestingly, Buckingham *et al.* (2013) argue that socio-economic status stands as a proxy for a range of other individual and school-based variables that are more likely to directly affect literacy. This constellation of factors offers an explanation of *Why poor children are more likely to become poor readers*. Although evidence for some factors is stronger than for others, the individual mediating factors that they identify are:

- early literacy ability such as oral language ability and phonological awareness;
- home learning environment, including encouragement of intellectuality and reading, development of self-regulation, and the number of books in the home;
- time spent reading outside school: the 'Matthew effect';
- physical health: poor health, including oral health, which affects school attendance;
- poor quality sleep;
- behaviour: behaviour problems predict low reading ability and vice versa.

School factors are identified as the material resources of a school, structural characteristics and school practices, including teacher quality and quality of reading instruction. In addition to this constellation of issues, Buckingham *et al.* (2013) argue that the evidence suggests that there is an interactive effect, that children from lower socio-economic groups are more adversely affected by these factors than their more advantaged peers – for example, poor quality sleep and school absenteeism seem to have a more detrimental effect on children from low socio-economic backgrounds. Importantly, they conclude that *at an individual level the impact of socio-economic status on school-age reading achievement seems to be largely exerted through its relationship with early literacy.*

(Buckingham *et al.*, 2013, p204)

Early years settings are therefore in a uniquely powerful position to support these children's literacy. We know that high-quality pre-school provision has a positive impact on children's later learning (Pascal *et al.*, 2013) and that skilled and knowledgeable staff are an important part of achieving this (Sylva *et al.*, 2003). So, as early literacy is vital for children's later learning, equally vital is practitioner's knowledge and understanding of young children, child development, early years pedagogical approaches, and practitioner's subject content knowledge, which in terms of literacy includes a good understanding of what leads into literacy.

The pedagogy of early literacy: the adult's role in provision that leads into literacy

What the adults in a setting know and do is a significant aspect of high-quality early years provision. The Effective Provision of Pre-School Education (EPPE) study (Sylva *et al.*, 2003) was unequivocal in its conclusions that, pedagogically, provision that best meets the learning needs of young children is a balance of child-initiated and adult-focused activity, and this has become the accepted desirable pattern of adult provision and interaction in early years settings. The main focus of the adult role in early years provision should be engagement with children in the continuous free-flow provision in ways that support individual children's learning based upon clear formative assessment of their abilities and needs. This provision should be enhanced by adult planned and led activities that focus on specific knowledge and skills, again informed by formative assessment. The balance between the two will depend upon the children's abilities and needs, and will need to be monitored to ensure that provision is closely mapped to the needs of each particular group of children. This approach is the same for early literacy as for all other areas of learning: children need the freedom to play and interact in activities that embed literacy practices in meaningful and purposeful ways, alongside knowledgeable and skilled adults who support their learning through playful interactions that may include commentary, discussion, questioning, pondering and direct teaching.

It is important to be aware that the balance of child-initiated play and adult-focused activity is a contested area. The government's focus on early years as a way of ameliorating later problems with learning has led to significant concerns about the 'schoolification' of early years provision. Pedagogically, the concern is that children will be required to spend more and more time involved in adult-led, outcomes-focused activity rather than play-based, child-initiated activity. This debate is particularly relevant to phonics teaching, with significant concern about a persistent pull towards school-based, formal, teacher-led teaching of phonics in early years. We know that this is not appropriate for most young children, so early years practitioners and teachers need to have a clear understanding of what comes before phonics and the pedagogical practices that enable children to develop the knowledge, skills, understanding and attitudes that lead into literacy in ways that enable children to come to formal teaching with a strong chance of success.

Claims for this play-based approach also have implications for the role of the adults, both in their understanding of the processes and their pedagogical approach. Within the field of early years research, important questions have started to be asked about the precise nature of child-initiated play and the adult's role in this (Broadhead, Howard and Wood, 2010). This research and commentary is undertaken within a commitment to current early years pedagogical practices, with the aim of developing practice through a more sophisticated understanding of the processes. For example, Kalliala (2013) challenges what she sees as the over-generalisation in our understanding of 'the competent child' in child-initiated play. Her close observation of children shows children who are *eager to learn, are competent and strong, but also vulnerable, immature and needy in different respects* (Kalliala, 2013, p4), and notes that differences between individual children are remarkable. She comments that seeing children as 'competent social actors' was a step forward in how children's learning is viewed, but that it risks becoming a taken-for-granted pedagogical assumption that does not perhaps reflect what is actually happening in early years settings. Kalliala concludes with a call to open up our understandings of children.

> *When we are open to examples that challenge the cherished idea of children as competent social actors, we find a rich variety of both more competent and less competent children who need adults in many ways.*

(Kalliala, 2013, p14)

In doing so, she argues, we recognise the impact that this may have on espoused theories that underpin our pedagogical practice. Wood (2014) also argues that we need to be more aware of precisely what is happening in children's play, to better understand and respond to children's actual abilities and needs. Her paper below outlines a research project that, similarly to Kalliala (2013), urges us to look very closely at the dynamics of children's play in settings, and recognise that there are aspects of free choice and free play that serve to advantage some children and disadvantage others.

WHAT DOES RESEARCH TELL US?

Free choice and free play in early childhood: troubling the discourse (Wood, 2014)

Wood's study (2014) aimed to ask questions about the ways in which we see and understand free play in early childhood: the discourse. She argues that it is important that we continue to question the taken-for-granted assumptions about play in early childhood and reconsider what we do and why in the light of research evidence that is sometimes uncomfortable and challenging to the established discourse.

(Continued)

Wood (2014) argues that the established discourse of child-centred education makes universal assumptions about young children's abilities to engage in free play and free choice, and therefore to benefit from the learning opportunities embedded in the activities and experiences: she asks who is, and in what ways are some children, advantaged and others disadvantaged by this approach. She highlights a range of studies that identified variations in what, and whose, choices are allowed and restricted – for example, rough-and-tumble play and 'aggressive' play (Jarvis, 2007). Thus, she argues, that children's agency in the choices that they make are different from those sanctioned by adults or advocated with a child-centred discourse.

Wood's (2014) study therefore aimed to document and critically examine children's individual and group choices during periods of free play, and to reveal how the social dynamics of power operate within different contexts.

The study involved 48 hours of running record observations of 10 children who formed an established and experienced morning Foundation Setting group. All were aged between 3.10 and 4.5 years old.

In accordance with other research, Wood (2014) found that there was variation in the ways in which children engaged and were able to engage with the activities and experiences provided.

- *How children enacted agency in their play*. She observed children who challenged the rules of the setting, using subterfuge and strategies to circumvent rules – for example, standing on blocks to make themselves taller so that they could build higher and higher towers of bricks and still meet the safety rule for block play of not building higher than their tummy buttons.

- *The ways in which children sought adults' assistance, attention affirmation and support*. Wood (2014) observed many examples of children's obvious engagement, enjoyment and involvement in adult-focused and planned routinised activities, and contends that although these activities are often noted as interrupting children's free play, the well-being of the children was evident in their relationships and interaction with the adults at these times.

- *Inclusion and exclusion*. Wood (2014) observed that strategies for joining in play activities had to be learned and earned. Some children were included at times and not at others; some inclusion in play was partial, and at times some children chose to exclude themselves from play with others, happy to engage in solitary activity despite attempts from other children to engage them in play.

- *Whispering* was another aspect of children's awareness of strategies for inclusion and exclusion, some children whispering as part of friendship patterns to control who and what others heard. Wood notes that this involved complex interpersonal and intersubjective skills, and these were crucial to determining whose choices took precedence and how play was managed, in particular who could enter the play and who could be involved.

(Continued)

- *Frustration and resolution.* Wood (2014) concluded that success in resolving frustration seemed to be related to children's physical and social skills, mood and emotional competence. She notes (p12) that whether or not children limit or sustain their involvement with peers may be linked to task difficulty, specifically the extent to which children are able to manage and orchestrate the different elements needed to sustain play.

- *Silence.* Observations revealed several instances of children using silence as a way of excluding themselves or others from play, which Wood (2014) interprets as a power effect of choice and agency.

- *Walking, running and observing.* Children were observed moving between running, walking and observing in pairs, groups and alone, chatting, choosing and checking. Choices to do this were both intentional and opportunistic.

These analyses of the children's engagement demonstrate some of the ways in which free choice was exercised by the children. These choices involved different forms of agency, such as pretence, managing task difficulty, negotiating power dynamics and orchestrating individual and group activities (p14). It reveals how children are social actors with capabilities to create and interpret their social and cultural worlds. These complex processes, Wood (2014) concludes, involve more than a child's natural motivation to play, or their developmental needs: children use free play and free choice for their own purposes and this often has implications for others.

Thus, Wood (2014, p16) concludes that if spontaneous and responsive pedagogies are to be sustained in early years, educators need to be aware of children's repertoires of choice, specifically the ways in which freedom to choose may advantage some and disadvantage others.

In addition to their conclusion about pedagogical practices in early years the EPPE study (Sylva *et al.*, 2003) concluded that the quality of staff in a setting also had an impact on children's learning. Thus, early years practitioners and teachers need a high level of knowledge and skill to enable them to provide effective provision for our youngest children. This includes both high levels of pedagogical skill and a deep understanding of the content of what is being taught. In the context of this book, this would be a high level of understanding about how children learn, and a deep understanding of how children become literate, which includes knowledge of what comes before phonics. Perhaps most importantly practitioners and teachers need to know how to bring these together in ways that make learning meaningful for very young children. Shulman (1986) refers to this as Pedagogical Content Knowledge – *how* to teach and *what* to teach. He argues that skilled teaching happens at the intersection of pedagogy and content.

Thus, if we are to provide high-quality early years provision that successfully leads children into becoming literate, it is vital that the earliest stage of a child's journey is appropriate both in the content and the pedagogy. It is also essential that early years staff are skilled and knowledgeable in bringing these two aspects of teaching together to create developmentally appropriate early literacy experiences.

Schulman's notion of pedagogical content knowledge is highly significant in the strong emphasis on phonics in the teaching of early reading. The tensions and debates around early literacy are essentially around these two aspects: what is appropriate for very young children to learn and how should this be taught? There is significant concern in the early years sector about the persistent pull towards teaching phonics at an increasingly earlier age using a formal teacher-led approach. House (2011) refers to this as *Too Much, Too Soon?* This strong emphasis on phonics has resulted in many practitioners and teachers having good professional knowledge and understanding about the content and pedagogy of formal literacy teaching, but considerably fewer opportunities to become knowledgeable and skilled about what comes before phonics. The following chapters in this book aim to answer these questions about the content and the pedagogy of what comes before phonics.

Conclusion

This chapter has looked at the broader issues that lead into literacy learning. It has considered experiences in the home that shape and influence children's literacy development and ways in which settings can provide an appropriate early literacy learning environment. It has discussed the 'Matthew effect' and identified what we know about Why *poor children are more likely to become poor readers* (Buckingham *et al.*, 2013). The chapter has discussed the role of the adult in meeting children's needs in settings: a focus on deepening our understanding of what is happening in child-initiated play and the consequences this may have for some children and for our pedagogical practice; and a recognition that high-quality provision requires staff in early years to have strong pedagogical content knowledge.

References

Adams, MJ (1990) *Beginning to Read: Thinking and Learning About Print.* London: MIT Press.

Basit, TN, Hughes, A, Iqbal, Z and Cooper, J (2015) The influence of socio-economic status and ethnicity on speech and language development. *International Journal of Early Years*, 23(1): 115–33.

Broadhead, P, Howard, J and Wood, E (eds) (2010) *Play and Learning in the Early Years.* London: SAGE.

Buckingham, J, Wheldall, K and Bearman-Wheldall, R (2013) Why poor children are more likely to become poor readers: The school years. *Australian Journal of Education*, 57: 190.

Clay, M (1991) *Becoming Literate: The Construction of Inner Control.* London: Heinemann.

Dooley, C and Matthews, M (2009) Emergent comprehension: Understanding comprehension development among young literacy learners. *Journal of Early Childhood Literacy*, 9(3): 269–94.

Edwards, C (2014) Maternal literacy practices and toddlers' emergent literacy skills. *Journal of Early Childhood Literacy*, 14(1): 53–79.

EEF (no date) Education Endowment Foundation. Available online at: **https://educationendowmentfoundation.org.uk/about/** (accessed 11 September 2016).

Gray, C. and MacBlain, S (2015) *Learning Theories in Childhood*. London: SAGE.

Hartas, D (2011) Families' social backgrounds matter: Socio-economic factors, home learning and young children's language, literacy and social outcomes. *British Educational Research Journal*, 37(6): 893–914.

Harvard University Center on the Developing Child (ND) Brain Architecture. Available online at: http://developingchild.harvard.edu/science/key-concepts/brain-architecture/ (accessed 11 September 2016).

House, R (2011) *Too Much, Too Soon? Early Learning and the Erosion of Childhood*. Stroud: Hawthorne Press.

Jarvis, P (2007) In Wood, E (2014) Free choice and free play in early childhood: Troubling the discourse. *International Journal of Early Years Education*, 22(1): 4–18.

Kalliala, M (2014) Toddlers as more and less competent social actors in Finnish day care centres. *Early Years: An International Research Journal*, 34(1): 4–17.

Marsh, J (2003) One-way traffic? Connections between literacy practice at home and in the nursery. *British Educational Research Journal*, 29(3): 369–82.

Melhuish, E, Phan, M, Sylva, K, Sammons, P, Siraj-Blatchford, I and Taggart, B (2008) Effects of the home learning environment and preschool center experience upon literacy and numeracy development in early primary school. *Journal of Social Issues*, 64(1): 95–114.

NELP (2008) Developing early literacy. Available online at: www.nichd.nih.gov/publications/pubs/documents/NELPReport09.pdf (accessed 11 September 2016).

Pascal, C, Bertram, T, Delaney, S, Manjee, S, Perkins, M, Plehn, M, Bennett, A, Nelson, C, Razzak, S and Saunders, M (2013) The impact of early education as a strategy in countering socio-economic disadvantage. Research paper for Ofsted's Access and Achievement in Education 2013 Review. Available online at: www.crec.co.uk/docs/Access.pdf (accessed 11 September 2016).

Shea, M (2011) *Parallel Learning of Reading and Writing in Early Childhood*. London: Routledge.

Shulman, L (1986) Those who understand: Knowledge growth in teaching. *Educational Researcher* 15(2): 4–14. Available online at: http://itp.wceruw.org/documents/Shulman_1986.pdf (accessed 11 September 2016).

Stanovich, K (1986) Matthew effects in reading: Some consequences of individual differences in the acquisition of literacy. Available online at: http://people.uncw.edu/kozloffm/mattheweffect.pdf (accessed 11 September 2016).

Sylva, K, Melhuish, E, Sammons, P, Siraj-Blatchford, I, Taggart, B and Elliot, K (2003) The Effective Provision of Pre-school Education (EPPE) project: Findings from the pre-school period. Available online at: http://eppe.ioe.ac.uk/eppe/eppepdfs/eppe_brief2503.pdf (accessed 11 September 2016).

Wastell, D and White, S (2012) Blinded by neuroscience: Social policy, the family and the infant brain. *Families, Relationships and Societies*, 1(3): 397–414.

Wood, E (2014) Free choice and free play in early childhood: Troubling the discourse. *International Journal of Early Years Education*, 22(1): 4–18.

3 Speaking and listening

Introduction

Speaking and listening come before phonics. Talking and listening are the basis of much of our learning, in particular becoming literate. Children learn language. They learn it in their family and community, and it is developed later in settings and schools. Evidence shows that children's language ability is linked closely to their early language experiences.

This chapter explains how children acquire and develop language. Language learning for children who are growing up learning two or more languages is also considered. The chapter outlines the ways in which adults can support babies and young children's language acquisition and development, and considers the importance of non-verbal communication and children's silences in learning to talk and listen. The role of books, songs, rhymes, poems and language play are explored. These early essential skills are set in the context of phonics learning. Ways of working with parents in laying this important foundation for later phonics learning are also discussed.

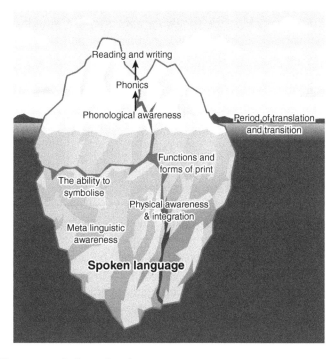

Figure 3.1   What comes before phonics

Speaking, listening and phonics

Spoken language, and the ability to listen carefully and respond, underpins what comes before phonics. Spoken language is the basis of all literacy learning, and a strong predictor of children's later school attainment (Basit *et al.*, 2015). Children need opportunities to learn language and, in their early years, opportunities to hear, use and practise it in a range of ways and in a range of situations.

How children acquire and develop language

As with all other understandings of children and their development, how children acquire and develop language has been explained in different ways. Different theories and explanations have, in their time, attempted to answer questions about how young children acquire language. The theories tend to reflect the wider context in which they were developed and are perhaps best understood as a developing story: a story in which each theory or explanation builds on and contributes to our current understanding of young children's language learning.

Behaviourism

An early explanation of how children acquire and develop language was Behaviourism. A behaviourist explanation of language acquisition applies the principles of reinforcement to language learning. Language learning is understood in the same way as all other learned behaviours: a process of stimulus and response. In this theory, language is learned and shaped through external reinforcement. It is understood as small steps towards speaking, encouraged through responses from other people. For example, a child babbles 'mamamama' and the response from parents and other adults assumes that this is an attempt at saying mummy and they demonstrate their delight at this. This delight acts as positive reinforcement, which encourages the child to repeat that sound and to engage in the dynamic of making sounds and receiving positive feedback. The child is seen as relatively passive in this process in that other people shape what the child learns through reinforcing that which they wish to continue.

A behaviourist understanding of language learning was, in its time, in line with other explanations of how humans learn. It emerged as part of the behaviourist school of psychology through the work of theorists such as Pavlov, Watson, Thorndike and Skinner. Their work was predominantly experimental laboratory work with a focus on how animals and humans behave rather than how they think or feel. In their experiments they showed that they were able to influence behaviour by linking a stimulus to a response. A behaviourist approach understands language learning in this same way: children produce 'language behaviours', other people respond, and this creates a stimulus-response dynamic which moulds and shapes the child's language.

Critics suggest that Behaviourism has limitations in fully explaining how children learn, and learn to use, our complex language system. Knowledge of young children's speech suggests that language learning goes beyond basic reinforcement of utterances. There are a number of reasons for this:

- the volume of language that we need to enable us to communicate and learn is huge and complex, so it would be impossible to reinforce each individual utterance for each child;

- we create and use innovative and, at times, unique language which hasn't been reinforced;

- children use words incorrectly that they don't hear and aren't reinforced, words such as 'treeses', 'wented' and 'swimmed'.

Behaviourism is, therefore, unlikely to fully explain how we learn language although, as Whitehead (2010) suggests, it may have some part to play in the initial stages of language acquisition, in learning and extending vocabulary, and in developing phonological awareness (*see* Chapter 8).

Nativism

The Nativist view of language acquisition emerged, in part, from interest in the question of how we acquire language that we are not directly taught. Nativists argued that even the most straightforward observation and analysis of children's language shows that they learn and use complex language structures with only limited direct instruction and reinforcement. Additionally, language is learned from rather imprecise language use from the people around us. Language acquisition is also universal: all people, without specific language learning problems, learn to speak. They concluded that the Behaviourist explanation of language acquisition was too simplistic to explain the complexity and universality of language acquisition.

One of the most influential people in developing and articulating a Nativist view of language acquisition was Noam Chomsky. Chomsky's work focused on the structures of the mind that enable us to learn language. He was interested in understanding how young children process the language that they hear. Chomsky proposed the idea of a 'Universal Grammar'. He argued that certain aspects of our knowledge and understanding, including language, are genetically determined. Universal Grammar is one such potential that we are born with and that develops over time through genetic unfolding. Chomsky argues that we are all born with the same potential to acquire language and this develops into knowledge of the particular language, or languages, to which we are exposed. This innate potential that makes language learning possible is referred to as a 'Language Acquisition Device' (LAD). This LAD enables us to abstract the governing rules of the language, or languages, that we hear (or see) and to generate utterances in that language (Smidt, 2011). Language learning is thus considered to be essentially an autonomous, internal, individual process. It is a process in which language acquisition is understood as being built from grammatical rules into communication. This LAD, Chomsky argued, offers an explanation for how children acquire complex language systems and for the universality of language acquisition.

Similarly to the Behaviourists, the work of Chomsky and other Nativists advanced the understanding of language learning, but left some important questions unanswered. Chomsky has been criticised for an over-emphasis on grammar and structure in language, rather than meaning. Critics argue that the most important function of language is to create meaning in a social world; that language acquisition is essentially a social, communicative process rather than an internal, structural, linguistic process. Thus, Chomsky, in focusing on structure and disregarding the importance of meaning, fails to take into account the most important aspect of language learning: it is a social process in a social world. This critique of a Nativist view of language acquisition and development was part of a wider movement in psychology, focused on the social aspects of learning strongly influenced by the work of Urie Bronfenbrenner. Bronfenbrenner proposed that children's experiences in the social world in which they lived and grew were highly significant in their learning and development. His *Ecology of Human Development* (Bronfenbrenner, 1979) demonstrated the significance of immediate and wider social environments on learning and, although he did not focus specifically on language development, his theory regarding the impact of social experiences on learning was highly significant in developing emphasis on social interaction in learning.

Social interactionism

The work of Lev Vygotsky and Jerome Bruner was influential in addressing the Nativists' over-emphasis on structure and grammar, and developing our understanding about the significance of social interaction in language learning. They revealed the intense social nature of language acquisition, starting from a baby's seemingly innate drive to communicate with others. This focus on social interaction does not preclude the notion of genetic inheritance, but emphasises a different function and aspect of language learning. Language learning from this perspective is understood as communication-driven and socially-shaped: the drive to acquire language is to enable us to communicate with others, and how we know, use and develop language is dependent upon our experiences in the social world.

Lev Vygotsy's work, emphasised the importance of the social world in children's development. He argued that it is through others that we become ourselves. It is in our interactions with others that we create who we are, and it is the cultural tool of language that expresses this in communication and articulates it in thought. Vygotsky's work focused on the importance of the social context in language acquisition rather than the processes involved. The main premise of his work is that as humans we have a range of psychological tools that enable us to use and extend our mental abilities. These tools are symbolic systems that we use to interpret and communicate reality, and include signs, symbols, plans, numbers, musical notation, charts, models, pictures and, above all, language (Dolya, 2010). These tools are developed in families and communities and become part of the culture which is then passed on to children as they grow and learn. For Vygotsky, language is the pre-eminent cultural tool and it is vital because of the interrelationship between thought and language. Language, he argues, forms the basis of thought. This means that the development of thought is closely linked to a child's language ability. This ability is in turn dependent upon the sociocultural context in which the child is acquiring and developing their language.

Jerome Bruner's significant contribution to our current understanding of language acquisition was his addition of a LASS to Chomsky's LAD. Bruner was concerned that Chomsky paid little, if any, attention to the role of interaction in language learning. Bruner's Language Acquisition Support System (LASS) aimed to address this. He argued that in order for the Language Acquisition Device (LAD – *see* Chomsky, above) to develop, children who are learning to speak need to be involved in clear, predict-able and repeated interactions with others. This social interaction, in all its forms, is the Language Acquisition Support System. Bruner's work on language acquisition is part of his wider understanding that learning is an active process in which learners are engaged in constructing new ideas and concepts. This construction of ideas and concepts is supported by more knowledgeable adults who scaffold the learning in a way that is appropriate to the learner's current state of understanding. In language acquisition, Bruner agrees that there must be an innate linguistic capacity that ena-bles the child to construct the grammar, but children are able to acquire this grammar effectively because the people around them create a meaningful world of interaction. Children's daily routines, interactions and play provide the framework for this inter-action in which the meaning is indicated by the context; this LASS to accompany Chomsky's LAD is, in Bruner's view, how a child acquires language.

Usage-based model

Tomasello (2003) further develops the idea of language acquisition as a social process in his 'usage-based model' of language acquisition. His argument turns Chomsky's notion of a universal grammar on its head. For Tomasello, language acquisition and develop-ment flow from communication to rule-based grammar. This is in contrast to Chomsky who sees language acquisition as building from grammatical rules to communication. Tomasello argues that language structures emerge from language use. The symbolic and representational dimensions of language occur first, as we communicate with others, and grammar is derived from these communicative utterances. Hansen (2010) describes this succinctly: the linguistic (Chomskian) hypothesis is that the small child understands words, and thereby decodes contextual meaning. The usage-based hypothesis is that the small child decodes contextual meaning and thereby understands words.

The basis of this patterning of language structures from communication is, in Tomasello's view, integrated with other cognitive and social-cognitive skills. He argues that these more general cognitive and social-cognitive skills enable a child to pattern their communicative utterances into the structures of language – namely:

- intention reading;
- pattern finding.

Intention reading emerges at about 9–12 months of age and includes things such as:

- the ability to follow the attention and gestures of others;
- the ability to direct the attention of others by pointing, showing and using other non-linguistic gestures;
- the ability to learn the intentional gestures of others, including their communica-tive functions.

Intention reading skills are necessary for children as they enable them to acquire the appropriate use of communicative symbols which eventually lead to the use of more complex linguistic expressions and constructions.

Pattern-finding skills include:

- the ability to recognise categories of similar objects and events;
- the ability to form sensory motor schemas.

These skills are necessary for children to find patterns in the way adults use linguistic symbols in utterances to construct the grammar of a language.

Intention reading and pattern finding are, according to Tomasello, skills that enable children to construct grammatical structures from communicative interactions and utterances. This has important implications for early years practitioners as it adds significantly to our understanding regarding interaction with children pre-linguistically. A usage-based approach requires that we recognise and encourage attention-sharing and pattern-finding skills, and engage with these communicative symbols as an integral part of young children's language acquisition.

Early communication

Non-verbal communication

What Tomasello's usage-based theory articulates is the importance of what comes before spoken language, as it is clear that babies and very young children are able to communicate prior to developing spoken language. This communication is non-verbal, so relies on eye contact, touch, gesture and sounds such as gurgling and crying. This early communication is an essential part of language development as children learn to interact with others.

Bonds of attachment

Talking and singing to babies, along with early eye contact, gazing, holding and touching, particularly skin-to-skin touch, are ways in which parents and children can establish warm, responsive and loving relationships – this is part of creating a bond of attachment. Attachment is an emotional bond to another person. It emerges from the special relationship that involves an exchange of comfort, care and pleasure between a young child and their parents and/or other significant carer. The central tenet of attachment theory (Bowlby, 1953) is that mothers (or carers) who are available and responsive to their babies' needs establish a sense of security. The baby learns that the mother is dependable, which creates a secure base for the child to move out into the world and engage their exploratory impulses with confidence.

This bond of attachment is the basis of interaction. It starts with interaction through mutual gazing and becomes interaction through language. The emotional involvement that flows from a bond of attachment supports us in tuning into a child's needs and responding in a timely and appropriate way. This includes engaging with a young child in talk, singing, rhyming and language play that are necessary as a lead into speech.

Gesture in early communication

There is increasing evidence about the role of gesture in children's language acquisition and development. Gesture refers to a child's non-verbal communication; pointing, waving, clapping and whole body movement. A number of research studies have found that there is a relationship between babies' and young children's use of gesture and the development of language. Communicative gesture has been shown to be a good predictor of vocabulary size and of the development of receptive and expressive language (Desrochers *et al.*, 1995; Rowe *et al.*, 2009; Iverson and Golin-Meadow, 2005). Additionally, Tomasello (2003) in his usage-based theory of language acquisition would argue that the process of intention reading in gesture enables young children to acquire the appropriate use of communicative symbols, which eventually leads to the use of more complex linguistic expressions and constructions. As parents and practitioners, we therefore need to use and react to children's use of gesture, recognising it as an early communicative act that requires a fulsome response.

Our understanding of how children learn to talk is not yet definitive, although the basics are now understood, although we are rapidly developing a more nuanced understanding, in part due to the development of technology which has opened up new areas of research and understanding. However, what we know about language learning is that children learn language through the interplay of an innate capacity to acquire language and social interaction. Theoretically, this is articulated in Chomsky's claim of innateness and characterised in part by the work of the behaviourists who emphasised the importance of positive feedback, and importantly Vygotsky's and Bruner's work on social interaction. We have an innate capacity to acquire language, but it is through our interactions with others that we acquire and develop language, and the evidence is clear that our ability in language is contingent on social interaction. An often-referenced study that articulates this relationship between our language capacity and social interaction is Risley and Hart's (2006) study outlined below.

WHAT DOES RESEARCH TELL US?

The everyday experiences of American babies: discoveries and implications (Risley and Hart, 2006)

Risley and Hart's research (2006) confirms our theoretical understanding of the importance of social interaction in children's language acquisition and development. This piece of research is often referred to by its findings: 'The 30 million word gap'.

The study emerged from observations by the researchers who were working with young children in America in the 1980s. They worked in Headstart programmes – local early years programmes based on a national initiative designed to break the cycle of poverty by providing 15–20 hours per week of enriched early experience for children from poor backgrounds. They observed that this provision had not brought these children's attainment to the level of the average American child in later school success. This led them to consider what happens in the children's families. They worked out that by the time the children came into pre-school provision at three years old, they had had 15,000 hours of learning opportunities in their home. Risley and Hart (2006) wanted to know

(Continued)

how full or empty of learning experience were those hours of opportunity, and to compare the lives of babies from the poorest families with the lives of babies from working-class and professional families.

(Risley and Hart, 2006, p1)

The study consisted of observations of 42 babies from a range of different families: parents who were doctors, lawyers, office workers, manual workers and families on welfare (benefits). The researchers visited the homes each month when the children were aged between 7 and 36 months. They visited at different times in the day, evenings and at weekends when the babies were awake, and recorded everything said to the baby, all the talk that the baby overheard, and everything the baby did or said during an hour of daily life. They hoped to answer the question:

What actually goes on between American parents and babies in everyday family life while babies are learning to talk?

(Risley and Hart, 2006, p2)

The most important things that the researchers found surprised them.

1. A lot of talk goes on between average parents and typical infants and toddlers in everyday home life.
2. There are large and consistent differences between families in the amount of time, encouragement and talk given to their infants and toddlers.
3. 'Extra' talk is automatically more complex and positive.
4. Toddlers' talkativeness stops growing when it matches the level of their parents' talkativeness.
5. Expressive language practice is linked to receptive language experience.
6. The amount of family talk is a characteristic of low and high social class.
7. The amount of family talk accounts for children's vocabulary growth and related intellectual outcomes.

Risley and Hart (2006) concluded that:

This thorough and careful measurement of both language outcomes and language experience permitted the surprising discovery that the large differences in the amount of language experience that had accumulated before the children were three years old accounted for most of the equally large differences in vocabulary growth and verbal intellectual outcomes by age three – and many years later. By age three, some children were so hopelessly behind in total language experience and resultant total vocabulary size that no later preschool or school intervention could catch them up.

(Risley and Hart, 2006, p5)

Bilingualism: acquiring and developing two or more languages

Children are born into families and communities which all use language (spoken and/or signed). They acquire and develop their language knowledge and skill in this family and community. This means that children who grow up in families and communities in which there is more than one language spoken will acquire and develop the languages that they hear and that they use to communicate with people in their community. Many children growing up in the UK live in families and communities in which different languages are spoken. These children will either grow up, or become, bilingual or multilingual. Children who are bilingual live in two languages. Children who are multilingual live in more than two languages. This means that these children need to use more than one language to interact in their normal daily life in their family, their school and their community.

Some bilingual and multilingual children will learn English from birth alongside their home and community language(s) and so start in settings and/or in schools speaking both languages. Other children will learn and speak only their home and community language(s) at home and learn English when they come to nursery or school. Other children will come to live in England after they have learned their home and community language(s) in another country. These children may be in England temporarily, accompanying parents working or studying here, or as a refugee, or they may have come to live here permanently. These children will need to learn English when they start school in England to enable them to form and maintain friendships and to learn in school. In some countries, there are two official languages, so the whole country operates bilingually. For example, in Wales there are two official languages, Welsh and English. Both languages have equal status in law, so everything is provided and translated into both languages. This means that many children in Wales grow up living in two languages.

There can be little doubt that children who attend school in England need to know or learn English to access all that is on offer in settings and schools. However, this focus on the need for children to acquire English has, in the past, obscured the importance of valuing and supporting other language(s) that are spoken in homes and communities. This has begun to change and it is now recognised that, for children who speak languages other than English, English needs to be added to their repertoire of languages rather than home and community languages being replaced by English.

Learning English as an additional language

The same principles apply to acquiring additional languages as learning a first language: that children need to hear, use and practise the language in a range of ways and in a range of situations. When children who have yet to learn English come into settings and engage with experiences that enable them to begin to learn English, there is a series of stages that they are likely to go through. According to Tabors (1997), there are four stages.

1. *Children use their home language* Children coming into an environment in which a different language is spoken may use their home language initially with the expectation that they will be understood. This period is likely to be quite brief as children realise that they are not understood. The messages that they receive about the value of their home language are very important at this stage. It is important that their home language is valued and that they don't begin to believe that they must replace their home language with English – rather, that learning English will add to their repertoire of languages.

2. *A silent or non-verbal stage* Many bilingual and multilingual children, on entering an unfamiliar early years setting, will go through a period when they fail to interact verbally. They often continue to interact non-verbally (facial expressions such as smiles, gestures such as pointing) and spend time watching and listening intently to tune into the language around them. At this stage, children may be observed using English quietly to themselves – rehearsing the language that they are acquiring.

3. *Beginning to use English* Children begin to use single words, formulaic phrases and repetition during the earliest stages of learning English. Children often learn and use 'chunks' of language that they have heard – for example, parts of rhymes or songs, routine greetings or language used at specific times such as group times or registration.

4. *Producing and using English* With practice from opportunities to hear and use English, children will eventually begin to produce more complex language by building on and extending the 'chunks' of language that they are using. This may start by being single words or 'chunks' strung together to approximate to the intended meaning. Children need ongoing opportunities to hear English and appropriate opportunities to use their developing language to support this process of language learning.

It is important to be aware that these developmental patterns, like all developmental patterns, are guides only. Children will develop at their own pace and this will be dependent upon a range of factors. The pace of development will vary between children and for individual children – for example, one child may spend a lot of time watching and listening before very quickly moving into speaking in complete sentences, while another child may very quickly start using single words and stay at this stage for a long time. Additionally, the stages themselves are not discrete. Children are likely to move backwards and forwards between the stages depending on the context. Also, they may be operating at one or more stages at the same time according to the context in which they are using English. As practitioners, it is important that we observe children closely so that we are aware of children's changing abilities and needs, and match our provision and interaction to those abilities and needs.

Listening and silence

You can often observe very young children when absorbed in close attention to what is happening wholly engaged in the activity of watching and listening. In these moments they often seem physically 'paused' but highly alert to what is going on. Rogoff *et al.* (2003) refer to this as 'intent participation': learning through keen observation and listening in, in anticipation of later participation. They note that this way of learning is observable in young children's impressive and rapid acquisition of language.

Listening and silence are, therefore, important aspects of children's language acquisition and development. The silence that comes with listening carefully is vital for children to be able to tune into language(s) that they hear: the rhythm, pace, tone, intonation and stresses, as well as words and syntax, and situated ways of interacting and communicating. This is also evident in older children who are learning English as an additional language. As Tabors (1997) notes, a silent, listening period is an observable stage of learning an additional language, and it is to be expected as children absorb what they are hearing, and move into producing words and phrases in their new language.

All children, therefore, need opportunities to listen carefully – quiet times when they can attend to and absorb language. This may be listening to a story or discussion. It may be standing watching and listening to other children play, or observing other children singing or saying rhymes and poems. As Rogoff *et al.* (2003) comment, this way of children learning is often overlooked because practitioners tend to be familiar with other more direct, active pedagogical approaches.

Practitioners therefore need to facilitate times for children to stand and stare and absorb. This requires an awareness that children do not need to be active and moving, involved and contributing all the time; that the time and space to stand and observe in silence can be a powerful learning tool for young children.

Another important aspect of the ability to listen carefully is that it enables young children to attend and respond to what they hear. A child's ability to attend to the rhymes, rhythms and patterns in language is necessary to later learning, including phonics (*see* Chapter 8). The ability to listen, attend and tune into language is fostered by opportunities for engagement with language, such as stories, rhymes, songs, poems and language play.

Interaction to support babies and young children acquire and develop language

All the evidence we have on children's language acquisition and development points to the central role of interaction. This means that those of us who work with young children have an essential role to play in children's language acquisition and development.

At its most basic, talk can be used functionally – to ask for things, to protect ourselves, to issue requests and instructions, and this would probably be sufficient to function within society. But children who are learning language need more than this if they are going develop their language to its full potential. They need to engage with people who talk communicatively as well as functionally – people who use language to explain, to discuss, to explore, to imagine, to express ideas and thoughts, who play with language through rhymes, jokes and word play. Put simply, this means that we need to say more than is necessary. In addition, children need adults who listen carefully to them to tune in and adapt their interaction to their abilities and needs, and they need opportunities to engage in talking to practise and refine their developing language. Davidson and Snow's (1995) research, outlined below, evidences the powerful effect of a child's early linguistic environment on later reading skill.

WHAT DOES RESEARCH TELL US?

The linguistic environment of early readers (Davidson and Snow, 1995)

In this study, Davidson and Snow (1995) were interested in the socio-linguistic experiences of children who were early readers. They argue that

> *precocious reading acquisition is generally associated with the development of sophisticated verbal linguistic abilities but that no causal link has been found.*

> (Davidson and Snow, 1995, p5)

They cite a range of previous studies that indicate that it is certain types of linguistic skill that lead into early reading – namely, decontextualised language.

Their study, therefore, was an exploratory analysis of the language skills and language environment of precocious readers, focused on the oral decontextualised language and literacy skills. From these previous studies the team hypothesised that

> *The homes of precocious readers were expected to evidence an even richer language environment than those of children developing literacy at the expected pace, and the children in turn to display more advanced oral language skills.*

> (Davidson and Snow, 1995, p7)

> *(Continued)*

The study involved 12 children, six early readers and six pre-reader peers, with four boys and two girls in each group. All children met a range of criteria regarding their first language, family group, academic qualifications of parents, confirmation that children had not been in any reading acquisition intervention programmes and that they exhibited certain precocious reading skills. Data was collected through family videotaped interactions, child interview and a battery of standardised reading tests, including testing decontextualised language.

Outcomes of the study confirmed that all the children in these families had sophisticated language skills in terms of speech complexity, conversational exchange, level of topic complexity in conversation and topic initiations. The study showed that all the children had learned to talk in families where the parents used complex and sophisticated language, as they encouraged their child's language development, corrected their mistakes and used language for the discussion of complex matters. However, as anticipated, the study concluded that the language skills of the early readers were shown to be even more impressive in terms of the use of decontextualised language.

The authors conclude that while this may not show a causal link, there is sufficient evidence in their study to strengthen the argument that particular uses of language, evident in these families, are conducive to later literacy learning.

Practitioners can therefore best support children's language acquisition and development in three ways, by:

- saying more than is necessary;
- listening carefully;
- providing opportunities for children to engage in talking.

Saying more than is necessary

Practitioners need to use a range of strategies to ensure that they engage with children in ways that actively support and extend their language. So, how do practitioners ensure that they say more than is necessary? What characterises interaction that goes beyond the functional use of language and engages children in effective interaction?

High-quality adult–child interaction in a setting
Evidence shows that there are certain features of interaction with young children that best support their learning (Neaum, 2005).

Playfulness
One of the defining characteristics of positive interaction is playfulness – interaction in which practitioners clearly enjoy the processes of being engaged with the children in their talk and learning, where practitioners are lively and enthusiastic in their interactions with children.

Commentary

This means talking about the activity or experience as it is happening. The talk can be used to comment, explain, interpret or clarify. The important thing is that children are hearing language used to mediate their experience. Through commentary, language is used to refer to a real experience in an authentic situation. Commentary can be used in a number of ways.

1. To articulate the observable processes in an experience or activity. For example: I can see that you are ...' or 'it's interesting how you ... ' . In this way, the child is given access to the language associated with the experience or activity, and to how we use language for thinking through the interpretation or explanation of what is happening.

2. To reflect back the child's learning and/or make links between what the child is currently engaged in and prior learning. For example: 'Ooooh good thinking ... Let's look inside this box and see if you have listened carefully to the clues and worked out what's hidden in there ... Can you remember last week when we were trying to work out what was in that tiny box and we thought that it was a ring, because the clues were that it was shiny and you wore it on your finger ... Let's see if we're right this week ...'

In this way a child has access to language associated with the activity, and a model of how language can be used to link different aspects of activity and learning across time and space.

3. To articulate the adult's thought processes while engaged in an activity or experience or just alongside a child. For example: 'I was just wondering which book to read at storytime today, I love this one, but I think it is too long for my group so I'm going to look for a shorter one ... one about animals I think, because it is our week to look after the rabbits so we've been talking about animals and what we need to do to look after them.'

In this way, children are exposed to language for communication and thinking. They hear the thoughts that usually happen silently in our heads as we think things through. This broadens the range of language that they hear, and models the way that we use language for thinking.

Teachable moments

These are moments when a practitioner notices that a child is ready to learn something and seizes the moment to teach the child, and so move the child's learning forward. It relies on the practitioner being able to notice and use moments as they arise to engage with the child to support their learning. Teachable moments can be used specifically to teach language – for example, vocabulary, or to model appropriate language usage or language for thinking, and to teach aspects of early literacy, including phonics. For example, developmentally appropriate teachable moments may be articulating the letter sounds as you read labels on toy boxes when tidying up, or encouraging a child to articulate the initial sound in their name when you write their name on their painting.

Scaffolding and extending talk

Scaffolding is a term coined by Bruner to explain the adult's role in supporting children's learning. He uses the image of the adult's provision and interaction acting like a scaffold that is built around the child while they are learning. Once the child has acquired the knowledge, skill or understanding, the scaffold (adult support) can be removed. The scaffold is then put in place for the next stage of learning. Adults can scaffold children's talk by adopting interactive practices that encourage engagement in talk – interactive strategies that offer opportunities for the child to hear and respond to talk and for them to engage in interaction. These include:

- discussing;
- pondering;
- questioning;
- modelling;
- introducing relevant vocabulary.

All these strategies that scaffold and extend language learning require practitioners to engage in interaction with children. At best, they require sustained interaction between adults and children, which is likely to result in interaction that requires saying more than is necessary.

Listening carefully

During activities practitioners need to be alive and sensitive to children's interests, abilities and needs. Interaction that engages children and results in effective interaction will need to be enjoyable and of interest to the child. Therefore, to encourage sustained interaction practitioners need to listen carefully and engage with what interests the child. This may involve listening carefully so that provision has opportunities for play and learning based on a child's interests, or it may involve listening carefully and following the child's lead during interaction. Positive interaction with children is characterised by a sharing of the pace, timing and direction of interaction between adult and child, so that both the practitioners and children contribute to the understanding of the interaction, activity or experience: they construct their understandings together (Neaum, 2005). Additionally, listening carefully is important so that interaction is contingent on the child's current level of language ability, and takes into account what knowledge and skill the child needs to develop next. By listening carefully, practitioners can adjust their interaction to meet the child's language needs.

Silence

As well as talking and listening to children, there is another dimension to the adults' role when interacting with children: silence. The role of silence also needs careful consideration when working with young children. Spyrou (2016) refers to the skill of tuning into the meaning behind children's silences as recognising the fullness of children's voices. Language is on a continuum from silence to voiced utterances, and each aspect of this communication continuum holds meaning, so attending to silences as a form of communication engages us with the complexity of young children's communication. Spyrou encourages us to observe and think carefully about what children are communicating through their silence, and what this means for our approach and interaction with them.

Providing opportunities for children to engage in talking

Our understanding of how children acquire and develop language means that they must have opportunities to use language as well as hear it (Saxton, 2010). Therefore, in settings we need to provide opportunities that encourage children to use their emerging and developing language.

Settings need to plan their provision effectively to ensure that there are opportunities for the children to play and talk together with their peers and with practitioners. Careful thought about activities and experiences can create spaces and activities which stimulate talk and strongly encourage children to communicate.

For example:

- role play that requires interaction, such as a barber's or hairdresser's or a vet's practice, a baby clinic or fancy-dress shop;
- collaborative den building inside and out;
- use of interesting artefacts to provoke and promote discussion;
- using puppets;
- constructing waterways with tubes and piping.

Similarly, careful thought about where practitioners spend their time can provide opportunities for talk. It is important that the staff at activities are skilled in talking with young children and it is clear that their task is to engage children in extended talk. Evidence suggests (Tizard and Hughes, 2008; Dockrell et al., 2004; Ginsborg and Locke, 2002;) that the talk in settings and schools tends to be predominantly around managing activities and children's play rather than sustaining conversation that focuses on and results in learning. Therefore, clear planning that enables staff to focus on sustained talk with children, to support their language learning, must be an important consideration in the provision in settings.

Creating spaces in settings to develop speaking and listening

Elizabeth Jarman (n.d.) has developed some interesting work on creating Communication Friendly Spaces in settings. It flows from observation of learning spaces for young children in other countries such as Denmark and Sweden. She argues that the space in a setting can be organised in ways that encourage children to talk and to listen and so support the development of their language and communication. Speaking and listening, she argues, are encouraged by creating Communication Friendly Spaces within settings. There are a number of features of these spaces.

- A lack of extraneous stimulus. Practitioners are encouraged to create a calm environment through the use of muted natural colours for displays and resources, uncluttered wall and table-top displays and well-organised, readily available resources.

- As much natural light as possible.

- Gentle lighting, where lighting is needed, such as the use of fairy lights.

- Low levels of background noise.

- Creating enclosed 'den-like' areas inside and outside that provide spaces for children to go and talk, and read and play;

- Creating spaces that are specifically for talking and listening, such as a storytelling chair.

Interaction that supports bilingual children's language learning

In addition to all the strategies outlined above, teachers and practitioners can also support bilingual children's English language learning in the following ways:

- keep talking even when children don't respond;

- accept non-verbal responses;

- praise all efforts at verbal communication, however minimal;

- use clear, precise language spoken at a normal pace, pitch and volume, so that children begin to develop an ear for the sound of natural spoken English;

- interact in ways that encourage children to repeat words (or numbers);

- actively include children in group activities and experiences where they are hearing and responding to language.

Talking with babies

Language acquisition begins in the earliest days of life as parents communicate with their baby though smiling, gazing, singing and chatting. Instinctively, we enter into this social relationship with the assumption that the baby is interested in, and capable of, communicating with us. Indeed, we often engage with babies as if they are participating in the interaction by anticipating and modelling their contribution in the interaction. Babies respond reciprocally to these communicative acts in various ways: through becoming still and listening, through eye contact and gazing and, as they grow and develop, through whole body movements and vocalisations. This is evidence of a strong internal drive for babies to engage in communication and enter into social interaction. These powerful social communicative interactions are the beginnings of language acquisition and, if nurtured, will enable a child to acquire and develop spoken language with ease.

Positive strategies for talking with babies
Interaction requires that at least two people are engaged with one another. As babies have limited capabilities to initiate this interaction, it requires that other people

actively engage with the baby to support and develop their communicative skills. The National Literacy Trust's Face to Face research (2010) identified key areas that contribute to effective communication with babies and, although the study (NLT, 2010) was focused on parents, the same processes are effective for babies in day-care. They showed that effective communication practices with babies included:

- contingency: babies and parents or carers being 'tuned in' to reciprocal communication;
- the nature and types of parent–baby interaction.

Contingency

Contingency refers to the level of reciprocal communication produced in an interaction between baby and parent. It means that the parent and baby are fully orientated towards the interaction, that they are both cueing into and responding to one another.

These high levels of joint attention and reciprocity are associated with more effective communication and, in turn, with more rapid child language development. This synthesis of research evidence concluded that parents who take their lead from their child in this way are more effective than those who directed them, and that mothers who frequently respond verbally to their children's play and vocalisations supplied their children with more effective and nuanced language models than those who responded occasionally.

Effective interaction with babies

Some of the ways in which parents and babies interact have been shown to be particularly effective in supporting children's communication and language skills:

- gesture;
- meaningful interaction;
- use of an elaborated way of talking (saying more than is necessary).

Gesture is important. Gesture precedes language and is indicative of a baby's language and cognitive skill – for example, communicative pointing and waving bye-bye to a prompt. These early gestures have been linked with good receptive and expressive language development (National Literacy Trust, 2010). This requires that parents (and practitioners) are aware of children's use of gesture as a communicative act and that they respond accordingly. A response is required to enable the communication to be a successful two-way process, which will in turn encourage children to continue to use gesture to communicate as they move towards using spoken language.

Talk with babies that enhances communication and language skill is talk that has a meaningful context: daily events, interesting things that happen and recalling things that have happened. At its most effective, interaction with babies and very young children should explain and elaborate on routines and events, involve questions and seek to construct an understanding with the child. This more detailed interaction, rather than simply description, leads to more contextual information for the child, more use of questioning and a wider use of vocabulary. This means that the child is exposed to more language – more vocabulary and more complex language constructions – which in turn has an impact on children's language acquisition (NLT, 2010; Hart and Risley, 1995).

An elaborated style of talking which also combines a particular communicative style with detailed content has been shown to have an impact on children's language acquisition. An effective style of interaction is one in which the way that you speak is exaggerated: intonation, pitch, pace, facial expression are all made more dynamic in the interaction and words, and there is a high level of repetition and echoing of words, phrases and actions. This elaborated communicative style is sometimes referred to as 'motherese' or child-directed speech (CDS).

Interaction with babies in day-care
The same principles of what constitutes effective interaction with babies apply in day-care. Practitioners need to engage in meaningful, individually focused, recip-rocal communication. In day-care, this requires that the room and the staffing are organised to enable this to be an important part of each day. Practitioners need to be aware of the importance of communication with babies and young children, and plan time for talking, because there is a risk that in a busy day-care setting time to talk gets squeezed in alongside everything else and so takes place in unfocused short bursts as staff divide their time and attention between all the tasks that they have to do. Practitioners need to prioritise communicative interaction with individual children in which the pace, timing, direction and flow of the interaction is continually contin-gent on the baby or young child's interest, ability and need.

Similarly, staff need to provide a literate environment for the children in their care. As well as time to talk, this includes: providing play activities that enable and encourage talk and communication; engaging in singing and teaching children nursery rhymes; encouraging babies and young children to listen carefully by drawing their attention to sounds and modelling focused listening; and reading books and poems, telling stories and language play. All of these are crucial if children's language and com-munication skills are to thrive: babies and young children need to grow and develop within a literate environment in which focused, engaged talk that is sensitive to their changing developmental needs is an important part of each day.

The importance of books, songs, rhymes, poems and language play

An excellent way in which young children can hear, use, practise and manipulate lan-guage is through books, songs, rhymes, poems and language play. These interesting and enjoyable activities provide wonderful opportunities for children to engage with language in different ways which will enhance their language acquisition and devel-opment, and their comprehension skills.

To support their language acquisition and development and their comprehension skills, children need both early and ongoing exposure to books, rhyme poems and songs. First and foremost, these are a rich source of enjoyment; they open up experiences for children, are a source for the expression of a wide range of emotions, and are a strong connection to children's cultural and social heritages. In addition, they offer authentic ways for children to hear and use language. Books, rhymes, poems and songs extend and enhance children's language capability by encouraging focused listening and responding, alerting children to rhyme and rhythm in language, introducing vocabulary, engaging children in playing with words and syntax, and providing an opportunity to develop their pronunciation and fluency in speech.

Language play is similarly an enjoyable and effective way in which children can engage with spoken language to explore and manipulate it. We play with language when we manipulate it for fun, telling jokes or making puns, using irony or double meaning to produce a particular effect, often a laugh or groan. This language play breaks and bends the usual rules of language, although importantly, as Crystal (1998) points out, language play is not just a random use of language – it has a powerful communicative effect, and particular rules that govern what and how we play with language, and the response of others. This engagement involves listening carefully, and using and manipulating language creatively. Language play supports the development of spoken language in a range of ways.

- *It aids pronunciation* through a focus on the properties of sound, particularly rhyming sounds.

- *It helps with the acquisition of grammar*: through the focus on riddles, jokes and word play, children begin to understand some things about the structure of a language.

- *It supports semantic development*: play with words, puns, nonsense words and nonsense talk develops an understanding of the meanings of words, phrases and sentences.

In addition, it opens up children's range of language uses; it enables them to become consciously aware of meanings in words and phrases. It deepens their knowledge and awareness of the potential of language and supports meta-linguistic awareness (*see* Chapter 5) and the development of phonological awareness (*see* Chapter 8).

Books, songs, rhymes, poems and comprehension
Comprehension refers to the capacity to understand and make meaning of our experiences in the world. It is a vital skill in reading, as reading consists of both decoding the words on the page and understanding the text: this is referred to as the Simple View of Reading (*see* Chapter 1). The ability to comprehend and make meaning of words and language whether in language play or in narratives, emerges through meaningful experiences that stimulate the development and use of meaning-making strategies (Dooley and Matthews, 2009). In this context, the benefits of books, songs, rhymes and poems are twofold: they provide excellent opportunities for children to engage with broad aspects of meaning-making in their lives, and they begin children's journey into literacy by developing text-based comprehension skills necessary for reading.

Whitehead (2002), in her observations of a child's first three years with picture books, tracks a young child's emerging engagement with meaning in books. Whitehead observed that, in his early months, Dylan's responses to books were tactile, energetic, excited and physical, and that he delighted in the repetitive and dramatic sounds of book language. Then, as his first words emerged, at around 10 months, his responses were more of concentrated involvement and observable scanning of pictures and print, as he began to further engage with meaning in language, rhymes, songs and books. This meaning-making became evident in his recognition and pointing at familiar and loved items and characters, and in his physical movement and sounds in response to familiar rhymes in the books. By his second year, Dylan had developed preferences for a number of books, such as *We're Going on a Bear Hunt* (Rosen and Oxenbury, 1989) and could track and enjoy the storyline through the repetition of language, the rhymes and onomatopoeic words. By 20 months old, Dylan could respond with understanding to illustrations in books and was showing that he was making links between the books, songs and rhymes and experiences in his life, clearly evident in his interest in tractors and trains. Over the next year, continued engagement with books enabled Dylan to deepen his ability to make meaning of and from stories. This was evident in his ability to show empathy and excitement alongside the characters, to anticipate story lines and show preference for particular books. By the age of three, Dylan was able to make meaning and respond to a wide range of texts, in particular, books rich in factual information that developed his understanding of, and enthusiasm for *sharks, fish, whales, dolphins, dinosaurs, the fauna of America, Africa and Asia, tractors, trains, trucks, diggers, the moon, stars space and rockets* (Whitehead, 2002, p285).

Getting parents involved

In addition to provision in the settings, practitioners need to consider how they can work with parents to support them to support their children's language learning. The REPEY study (Siraj-Blatchford *et al.*, 2002) found that the best outcomes for children happen when settings support the ability of parents to provide a good home learning environment. This supports the view that what is important for young children's learning and development is not who parents are, but what they do. A good home learning environment for language learning is based on the same principles as effective setting-based pre-school provision: children need opportunities to hear and use language in a range of ways and in a range of situations. They need adults who say more than is necessary, who listen carefully and adapt their interaction to the child's abilities and needs, and provide opportunities for children to use their developing language.

The National Literacy Trusts Early Words Together (NLT, 2015) programme identifies a range of research evidence-based ways in which parents can support their children's developing language:

- sharing books and stories;
- singing songs and rhymes;
- playing with other children;

- playing with letters and sounds;

- painting and drawing;

- visiting the library;

- going out on trips and exploring the environment.

Schools and settings have a range of ways in which they encourage parents to become involved in these activities and ideas, both in the setting and at home, so that they become part of what happens in the family. Ideas for achieving this include:

- photos to hand to parents at the end of the session of their child engaged in an activity as a prompt for questions and conversation;

- written or recordable postcards to hand to parents at the end of the day that act as prompts for them to talk to their child about the day – for example, 'Ask me about the seeds that we planted today' or 'Today we about talked about the weather. I can tell you what I learned';

- recordable postcards:
  - for children to record songs and rhymes that they are learning to play back and go through at home;
  - for children to take home and alongside parents to briefly record things that have been done outside the school as a prompt to conversation at school;

- posts on social media to communicate what you have been doing in the setting to encourage parents to ask children about what they have been doing;

- posts on social media or posters in the setting that identify places to go and visit in the area and/or recommend children's comics and books, and/or identify good websites and/or electronic games for children to play;

- subscribe to children's comics, read them together in the setting and allow children to take them home;

- provide masks or hats that are linked to a story that children wear home, as prompts to discussion;

- toy libraries for children and families to borrow toys; book libraries; recorded stories with the accompanying book for families to borrow; DVDs of rhymes songs and poems and factual DVDs to borrow as prompts to discussion; story sacks and discovery sacks for children to borrow;

- stay-and-play sessions where parents can observe or join in with the activities;

- opportunities for parents to come into the setting and share their interests and expertise – for example, a parent may be able to come and cook with the children, or someone who works as a plumber can come and work with the children on constructing an outdoor waterway;

- if possible, visits to the child's home to read a book or play a game; even better, if you can leave the book or game with the child.

Many of the ideas above are suitable with small adaptations for children of all ages. It is also important to provide resources that all children and families can access, so this may mean having bilingual books and instructions for games and activities or bilingual staff who can provide resources in dual languages and support, and encourage families to become involved in the opportunities available. Additionally, you may need to consider parents' levels of literacy and provide information in appropriate ways that enables them to support their children's language acquisition and development.

Speaking and listening as the foundation of phonics

Children's spoken language and ability to listen and respond are the basis of almost all learning, including all later literacy learning. As Adams (1990, p294) observes, *all literacy is parasitic on language*. It is the pre-eminent tool that we have for thinking and communication. The ability to hear, use and manipulate language in increasingly sophisticated ways builds the foundation for all the knowledge and skills that are necessary to phonics learning. It lays the foundations for developing metalinguistic awareness as children use and manipulate language, and learn the language for talking about language (*see* Chapter 5). It is one of the earliest ways in which children engage in symbolic representation – for example, the sounds *d-o-g* blended into the word 'dog' to represent a four-legged, hairy, wet-nosed animal (*see* Chapter 7).

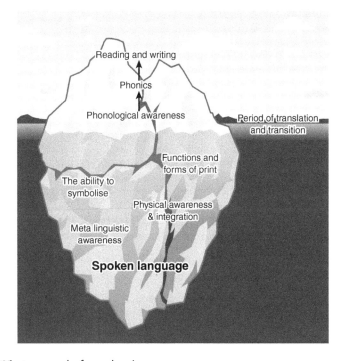

Figure 3.2   What comes before phonics

It leads into awareness of how we record language in print (*see* Chapter 6), and, being able to hear and discriminate between sounds and orally manipulate language is vital for the development of phonological awareness (*see* Chapter 8). All of this together, alongside physical development to support sensory integration and awareness (Chapter 4), forms a network of knowledge and skills that will enable children to come later to more formal phonics teaching ready to learn and with a high chance of success.

Conclusion

This chapter has focused on spoken language, a vital underpinning skill for learning including literacy and phonics. It has outlined the theoretical understandings of how we acquire and develop language, and linked these to other aspects of what comes before phonics. It has considered the issue of language learning for children who are growing up bilingual and the importance of early communication with babies. The chapter has discussed the significance of listening and silence in language learning, including the need for practitioners to be aware of this powerful way in which children learn. The chapter has considered the vital role of adults in children's language acquisition and development, and outlined positive interaction strategies for supporting children's language learning, including for children who are bilingual and babies. The importance of working with parents has been emphasised and ways in which this can be achieved outlined.

References

Adams, MJ (1990) *Beginning to Read: Thinking and Learning About Print*. London: MIT Press.

Basit, T, Hughes, A, Iqbal, Z and Cooper, J (2015) The influence of socio-economic status and ethnicity on speech and language development. *International Journal of Early Years Education*, 23(1): 115–33.

Bowlby, J (1953) *Childcare and the Growth of Love*. London: Penguin.

Bronfenbrenner, U (1979) *The Ecology of Human Development*. Cambridge MA: Harvard University Press.

Crystal, D (1998) *Language Play*. London: Penguin.

Davidson, RG and Snow, CE (1995) The linguistic environment of early readers. *Journal of Research in Childhood Education*, 10(1): 5–22.

Desrochers, S, Morosette, P and Ricard, M (1995) Two Perspectives on Pointing in Infancy. In National Literacy Trust (2010) Highlights from a literature review prepared for the Face to Face research project. Funded by the Department for Education's Children, Young People and Families Grant Programme. Available online at: **www.literacytrust.org.uk/search?q=face+to+face** (accessed 11 September 2016).

Dockrell, J, Stuart, M and Kind, D (2004) *Talking Time: Supporting Effective Practice in Preschool Provision*. London: Institute of Education.

Dolya, G (2010) *Vygotsky in Action in the Early Years*. London: David Fulton.

Dooley, C and Matthews, M (2009) Emergent comprehension: Understanding comprehension development among young literacy learners. *Journal of Early Childhood Literacy*, 9(3): 269–94.

Dudley-Marling, C and Lucas, K (2009) Pathologizing the language and culture of poor children. Available online at: **http://academic.evergreen.edu/curricular/med/langpoor.pdf** (accessed 11 September 2016).

Ginsborg, J and Locke, A (2002) Catching up or falling behind? *Literacy Today*, 32: 20.

Hansen, OH (2010) Usage based language acquisition in the Danish crèche. Paper presented at the OMEP World Conference, 11–13 August 2010.

Hart, B and Risley, T (1995) *Meaningful Differences in the Everyday Experience of Young American Children*. Baltimore, MD: Paul H. Brookes Publishing.

Iverson, JM and Golin-Meadows, S (2005) Gesture paves the way for language development. *American Psychological Society*, 16(5): 367–71. In National Literacy Trust (2010) Highlights from a literature review prepared for the Face to Face research project. Funded by the Department for Education's Children, Young People and Families Grant Programme. Available online at: **www.literacytrust.org.uk/search?q=face+to+face** (accessed 11 September 2016).

Jarman, E (no date) Communication Friendly Spaces. Available online at: **www.elizabethjarmantraining.co.uk/index.php?option=com_content&view=article&id=2&Itemid=6** (accessed 11 September 2016).

National Literacy Trust (2010) Highlights from a literature review prepared for the Face to Face research project. Funded by the Department for Education's Children, Young People and Families Grant Programme. Available online at: **www.literacytrust.org.uk/search?q=face+to+face** (accessed 11 September 2016).

National Literacy Trust (2015) Early Words Together. Final report. Available online at: **www.literacytrust.org.uk/assets/0002/6473/EWT_Final_Report-Impact_on_families_and_children.pdf** (accessed 11 September 2016).

Neaum, S (2005) Literacy, pedagogy and the early years. Unpublished thesis. University of Nottingham.

Risley, TR and Hart, B (2006). Promoting Early Language Development. In Watt, NF, Ayoub, C, Bradley, RH, Puma, JE and LeBoeuf, WA (eds) *The Crisis in Youth Mental Health: Critical Issues and Effective Programs, Vol. 4, Early Intervention Programs and Policies*, pp83–8. Westport, CT: Praeger. Available online at: **http://srdad.com/SrDad/Early_Childhood_files/Todd%20Risley.pdf** (accessed 11 September 2016).

Rogoff, B, Paradise, R, Mejia Arauz, R, Correa-Chavez, M and Angellilo, C (2003) First hand learning through intent participation. *Annual Review of Psychology*, 54: 175–203.

Rosen, M and Oxenbury, H (1989) *We're Going on a Bear Hunt*. London: Walker Books.

Rowe, ML, Sylva, K and Pugh, G (2005) Transforming the early years in England. *Oxford Review of Education*, 31(1): 11–27.

Saxton, M (2010) *Child Language: Acquisition and Development*. London: SAGE.

Siraj-Blatchford, I, Sylva, K, Muttock, S, Gilden, R and Bell, D (2002) Researching effective pedagogy in the early years. Research Report RR356. DCFS.

Smidt, S (2011) *Introducing Bruner*. London: Routledge.

Spyrou, S (2016) Researching children's silences: Exploring the fullness of voice in childhood research. *Childhood*, 23(1): 7–21.

Tabors, P (1997) *One Child, Two Languages: A Guide for Preschool Educators of Children Learning English as a Second Language*. Baltimore, MD: Paul Brookes Publishing.

Tizard, B and Hughes, M (2008) *Young Children Learning* (2nd edn). London: John Wiley & Sons.

Tomasello, M (2003) *Constructing a Language: A Usage-based Theory of Language Acquisition*. London: Harvard University Press.

Whitehead, M (2002) Dylan's routes to literacy: The first three years with picture books. *Journal of Early Childhood Literacy*, 2(3): 269–89.

Whitehead, M (2010) *Language and Literacy in the Early Years 0–7* (4th edn). London: SAGE.

4 Physical foundations of literacy

Introduction

The two important messages of this chapter are that physical development is integral to learning, and that children do not learn to sit still by sitting still. Children need to move physically to develop a range of skills that are vital to learning. This is because to learn effectively we need to have control over our bodies to enable us to sit still, focus and concentrate. Physical activity also enables young children to develop skills that specifically support literacy learning, such as tracking, spatial awareness and bilaterality. To develop these necessary skills, young children need the time, space and a range of physical experiences to develop balance, proprioception and sensory integration.

This chapter looks at why physical development is integral to learning, and makes specific links between this and learning phonics. It identifies a range of physical activities

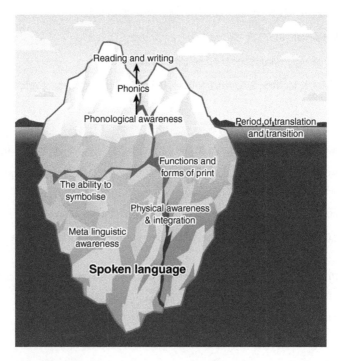

Figure 4.1 What comes before phonics

that develop and nurture these necessary skills. The importance of communicating this to parents and getting them involved in physical activities that lead into later literacy learning, including phonics, are explored.

Early physical development

In the first few years of life, children's physical development is prodigious. At birth, neonates have a series of primary reflexes that enable them to root, suckle, grasp, startle (Moro reflex), step and turn (tonic neck reflex). Motor development then occurs through skeletal and neuro-muscular maturation combined with physical interaction with the environment. This develops children's strength, control and dexterity, and they move from early uncoordinated activity to coordinated motor behaviour (Goddard-Blyth, 2011). For this to happen, children need opportunities for a wide range of physical activity, and with these appropriate experiences and the time and space to repeatedly practise, develop and refine their physical skills, children become increasingly physically competent. These physical skills are important in themselves, and children need appropriately challenging opportunities and experiences in their early years to move through the developmental stages. In addition, there is increasing interest and evidence of the impact that physical skills have on a child's ability to learn and to express their learning, as Goddard Blythe (2011, p. 131) notes, *throughout life movement acts as a primary medium through which information derived through the senses is integrated, and knowledge of the world is expressed.*

Why is physical development important to learning?

Learning is not all in the mind, but requires a range of physical skills, and evidence suggests that a number of these are highly significant in children's ability to engage in learning.

Balance and proprioception
Johnson (2014) highlights the importance of balance and proprioceptive systems in children's learning. First, she argues, children need to have a strong sense of balance both when moving and sitting still. Balance is controlled through our vestibular system which provides sensory information about motion, equilibrium and spatial orientation. Therefore, we learn to balance by moving, by getting a sense of our body in space and gaining control over it. Gaining balance is important, as once we have balance we can move more freely. This enables us to move and stay still without having to exercise conscious control over our bodies: our body is mind-free. It therefore follows that when children have had insufficient experiences for their body to be well balanced, they will need to think and concentrate on maintaining balance and uprightness; their bodies are not yet mind-free, and this can inhibit focusing on and attending to other things.

Closely linked to balance is a child's proprioceptive capability. Proprioception is the awareness of your body in space. For example, imagine that you are going to sit down on a chair. If you have sufficiently well-developed proprioceptive capabilities, you will be able to judge, without conscious thought, exactly where you are in space, where the chair is in relation to you, the movements that you need to make to sit down, including how much effort to use, and you will lower yourself precisely on to the chair. O'Connor and Daly (2016, p214) outline what having adequate development and integration of the proprioceptive system enables us to do.

- To 'feel' our bodies more accurately and to have the kind of body awareness that reinforces a sense of 'What do I look like?', 'Where do I start and finish?' and 'What does my body feel like?' both on the outside and the inside. This supports a subconscious sense of self as well as a physical body consciousness.

- To build spatial awareness of how our bodies 'fit' in the space around us.

- To efficiently process information about the relationship between different parts of our body (e.g. left and right, top and bottom, etc.) and how they can work together or separately.

- To manage strength and effort efficiently, in the way we interact with the environment, with other people and with objects.

- To navigate ourselves in the space around us and to plan movements.

Therefore, when our proprioceptive sense is adequately developed, our proprioceptors (sensory nerve endings located in muscles, tendons, joints and the vestibular apparatus) are constantly providing our brain with information about our position, and in doing so they reinforce the vital sense of feeling at home in our bodies, which leaves us free to focus on other aspects of our life (O'Connor and Daly, 2016). Thus, in order for children to sit still, pay attention and visually remember text-based information, they need good proprioceptive systems (Johnson, 2014). If these proprioceptive pathways have been allowed to develop fully, usually by the age of 7–8 years old, children's brains will have mapped their body and, importantly, the right and left side of their brains will be developing strong connections to one another. This bilateral integration will allow children to move both sides of their bodies at the same time, in concert or independently. Children's minds and bodies are deeply connected once they can proprioceptively perceive their bodies and have connected the right and left hand sides of their bodies together: they will have a full sense of their body in three-dimensional space (Johnson, 2014). Their minds will therefore no longer be needed to keep their body upright and balanced or to judge spatial distances, so their bodies will be mind-free, to pay attention, focus and learn (Pagini, 2012).

Neuro-motor integration
Goddard Blythe (2012) focuses on neuro-motor integration as an indicator of readiness to learn. She argues that a significant percentage of children in mainstream schools have been found to have immature motor skills and postural instability, and that this immaturity is rooted in the continued presence of a cluster of primitive reflexes. These reflexes are usually found in children up to six months of age, but are replaced over time as children mature and develop physically. Primitive reflexes develop in the womb and are there at birth to enable a baby to survive the early months of life, before connections to the higher centres of the brain are established. However, if they remain active longer than they should, these retained early reflexes

can interfere with the development of later reflexes and postural skills (O'Connor and Daly, 2016; Goddard Blyth, 2012). In support of this, Goddard Blyth (2012) cites a range of evidence including a longitudinal study published in 2010 that showed that children who failed to reach four key milestones in gross motor development at nine months old were found to be on average five points behind on cognitive tests at five years old. This led to the conclusion that *delay in gross and fine motor development in a child's first year were significantly associated with cognitive development and behavioural adjustment at five* (Goddard Blythe, 2012, p.5). While Goddard Blythe (2012) recognises that educational failure is a complex and multifaceted issue, she argues that many of the issues that are correlated with educational failure are beyond teacher and practitioner influence, issues such as the child's background, school attendance and learning difficulties, whereas enhancing children's physical development is a powerful way to support their learning, and it is both possible and developmentally appropriate.

Crossing the midline

Crossing the midline is another vital skill that occurs as a motor action and is integral to learning. The midline is an imaginary line that runs horizontally down the middle of our body, and 'crossing the midline' refers to any motor action that involves looking, reaching or stepping across this imaginary midline. Crossing the midline emerges as babies and young children develop bilateral integration: good communication between the left- and right-hand sides of the brain. Bilateral coordination is developmental: a series of progressive observable stages that emerge as children mature, alongside opportunities to move physically and handle and manipulate objects.

- Symmetrical movement: babies move their hands together in symmetry to reach and explore.

- Reciprocal movement: crawling, walking, running. These movements involve the body working in rhythm, with the same actions on one side, then the other.

- Asymmetric bilateral coordination: both sides of the body are working together doing complementary tasks; one side of the body is active and the other assists, for example, holding paper in one hand and using scissors to cut it with the other.

- Crossing the midline. One hand crosses over to the other side of the body to complete a task – for example, reaching over to pick up a block. Prior to this, young children tend to use their right hand for completing tasks on the right side of their body and vice versa. From this process most children develop a dominant side, often referred to as 'handedness' – whether they are right- or left-handed.

Children's ability to cross their midline is central to self-help skills such as getting dressed and brushing their hair, in physical activities that require looking, reaching or stepping across their midline, such as dancing, and bat and ball games, in supporting the development of a dominant side of the body, and later in becoming literate – for example, crossing the midline when tracking left to right to read and write (O'Connor and Daly, 2016).

Sensory awareness and integration

Sensory awareness and integration refers to children's ability to receive and respond to information gathered through their senses. It includes the five external senses – touch, taste, sight, hearing and smell – and the internal vestibular and proprioceptive senses: movement and internal body awareness (O'Connor and Daly, 2016). Sensory engagement shapes neural pathways and we build our understanding of the world around us as we make ever more complex connections based on previous experiences and sensations. Thus, babies and young children need rich sensory-motor experiences to build a strong foundation for later learning; they need to move to learn, to have the time, space and opportunities to take in information through their senses and piece it together. As Connell and McCarthy (2014, p. 53) observe, sensory integration *greatly affects not only what a child perceives but also how he interprets, understands and responds to sensory information – in other words, how he learns.*

Observable impact of immature physical skills

The evidence suggests that immature physical skills can inhibit learning in a number of ways. Children who cannot feel or perceive their body proprioceptively often need to move constantly, to seek external pressure to locate their bodies in space. This is manifest in a number of ways, wriggling when required to keep still, leaning on things, sitting on their feet or legs, or wrapping their legs around chair legs, to create sensory feedback to help their brains locate the position of their body. Their movements may be jerky rather than flowing, and can be impulsive or explosive at times (Johnson, 2014). These children may often be easily fatigued because of the work that they are having to do to keep their body upright and judge spatial distances. In addition, poor proprioception can also impact on the ability to fall and stay asleep as the body continues to seek external stimulation to feel and locate itself in space.

With particular reference to becoming literate, because these children find it difficult to locate their bodies in three-dimensional space (forwards, backwards, up and down, right and left) they may also have difficulties with perceiving and copying forms, such as letters, numbers and shapes, particularly those that have diagonal lines (Johnson, 2014). Goddard Blythe (2012, p8) concurs, noting that physical control and balance act as a reference point for cognitive operations in space including

> directional awareness (needed for way finding, understanding the orientation of symbols e.g. b and d, p and q, 2 and 5, and being able to read an analogue clock or compass), and mental operations in space.

This important relationship between physical skills and learning is evidenced in indications of positive outcomes where physical skills have been used as part of the remediation of learning difficulties. Reeves and Bailey (2014) undertook a review of research evidence on the effects of physical activity on children diagnosed with attention deficit hyperactivity disorder (ADHD). They analysed ten studies published since 2002 and found that *it can be plausibly claimed that physical activity interventions may provide an alternative approach to management of the disorder* (Reeves and Bailey, 2014, p10). Overall, the studies reported improvements in behaviour, increased attentiveness and improved cognitive functioning, and specific demonstrable benefits for specific subjects such as Maths and English. They concluded that the implications of this for schools (and settings) is that physical activity interventions should be considered as part of approaches to supporting learning for children with ADHD.

This area of study is still relatively new, so there is still considerable discussion about the exact relationship between physical movement and brain function (Archer and Siraj, 2015). However, with increasing concern about the appropriateness of current provision for our youngest children (Whitebread and Bingham, 2014), and recognised problems with children's levels of physical activity (British Heart Foundation (BHF), 2015), this area of research seems a very important addition to our professional understanding of how we can support young children's learning effectively and in developmentally appropriate ways.

WHAT DOES RESEARCH TELL US?

The quality of movement-play in early childhood settings: linking movement-play and neuroscience (Archer and Siraj, 2015)

Archer and Siraj's (2015) study was based on the increasing interest in the potential for neuroscience to enable us to understand learning in new ways. They argue that many are persuaded that there is a relationship between movement and brain stimulation, and so were interested in exploring the quality of movement-play in the early years.

They undertook a small-scale quasi-experimental study to investigate the quality of movement-play in pre-school settings. The study involved two intervention and two comparison settings. The quality of movement–play was assessed using the Early Childhood Environment Rating Scale – Extension (ECERS-E) (Sylva *et al.*, 2006).

Prior to the study, the scale was used to assess the quality of movement-play in all the settings. A notable item in both the comparison and intervention settings was a minimal or below score on the scale for adult engagement in movement with the children. This was interpreted as the practitioners adopting a non-interventionist observational approach. The intervention involved training for staff in the settings identified for intervention, which included discussion of how this could be implemented in the settings. The comparison settings did not receive this training. The rating scales were used again to assess the quality of movement-play following the intervention.

Findings for the intervention settings were positive, in contrast to the comparison settings whose scores remained the same. The intervention resulted in adults' scores on the rating scale for engagement increasing, indicating that they were more actively engaged in the children's movement-play. Additionally, Archer and Siraj (2015) found that, in the intervention settings, there was an increase in the variety of movement-play activities provided and, in some cases, children were experiencing more challenging and vigorous play.

They conclude that the literature informs us that this improvement in movement experiences for children should have an impact on their learning and development.

(Continued)

What is particularly important about their conclusions in the context of early literacy is that in the literature they cite the work of Goddard Blythe (2005) who has shown how interventions based on movements that occur in the first years of a child's life enhanced children's literacy skills. Thus, their findings can be used to support the arguments for a focus on sensory integration and awareness as an important aspect of what comes before phonics.

DEVELOP YOUR UNDERSTANDING

Look at the Harvard University Center for the Developing Child website. It cites evidence from neuroscience about the impact of young children's early experiences.

What does neuroscience tell us about the importance of a child's earliest years? What are the implications for staff who work with young children and their families?

Physical development and becoming literate

The general principle about the interplay of brain and body allowing children to be mind-free to focus on learning tasks applies to literacy learning in the same way as it applies to all other areas of learning: to learn, children need to be able to sit or stand still and concentrate. Their bodies need to be mind-free so that they can focus on the task in front of them. This requires that whole muscle groups work together to support their balance and postural control. So, children need to have developed good balance, coordination and proprioceptive capabilities before they are required to sit still, so that they come to learning capable of engaging with the learning. Pagini (2012, p102) concurs; her study concluded that *good motor abilities co-occur with better social skills and task-orientated behaviours in class*. These motor capabilities are developed, practised and refined through opportunities for physical activity: *children do not learn to sit still by sitting still*.

In addition, here are further reasons for just how important physical skills and integration are when learning to talk, read and write. As Goddard Blythe (2000) observes:

- eye movements and visual perception are linked to balance;
- speech is a motor movement that requires control of the mouth, tongue and lips;
- reading is an ocular motor skill;
- writing is a motor skill that involves coordination of the body and eyes, and is supported by the postural system.

There are clear links between balance and proprioceptive capabilities and literacy learning (Johnson, 2014; Pagini, 2012; Dolan 2000). Johnson (2014) argues that when proprioceptive pathways are fully developed children can look at shapes of letter (and numbers) and use their eyes to track the exact directions of the lines and curves, and are then able to form accurate mental images from this spatial information. In contrast, when children's eye-tracking and eye convergence are not fully developed, they are not yet ready to perceive and interpret this spatial information, and will often confuse and/or reverse letters and numbers. Additionally, Johnson (2014) argues that we often require children to hold a pencil and write before they are developmentally ready. Pencil grip is dependent upon proprioceptive abilities, and poor capabilities often result in a tense grip and cramped or incorrectly spatially organised writing. Johnson (2014) comments that she often observes young children being asked to write their name while they still have overflow movement in their other hand – the fingers of the non-writing hand are mapping the movement in the writing hand. This occurs when the child's vertical midline is not fully integrated because they have not fully developed bilateral integration pathways between the left- and right-hand sides of the brain.

Specifically with regard to phonics, Johnson (2014) argues that our current educational system is teaching children to read in a way that does not make sense developmentally. Reading, she argues, occurs when children can form and create mental pictures in the right-hand side of their brains while simultaneously decoding the corresponding word(s) with the left-hand side of their brains. (These assertions concur with the simple view of reading that there are two dimensions to reading: decoding and comprehension – *see* Chapter 2). However, one of the developmental effects of children being required to read ever earlier is that they do not have the necessary access to both sides of their brains; that they are being expected to read words when only the right side of their brains are developed. This means that they are having to use the right-hand side of their brains to recognise words rather than form mental images and scenes associated with the words that they are reading. In contrast to our current 'earlier is better' approach to teaching phonics and reading, she argues that it is not until around the age of 6½ years old to 7½ years old that the brain is developmentally able to *hear separate sounds within a given word and string the individual sounds together to sound out words phonetically* (Johnson, 2014, p5). Johnson's position, that we need to work with children at their developmental stage rather than focus on chronological age-based curriculum requirements, is supported in Goddard Blythe's (2000) paper below that outlines the link between motor skills and children's readiness for the demands of schooling.

WHAT DOES RESEARCH TELL US?

Early learning in the balance: priming the first ABC (Goddard Blyth, 2000)

In her paper, Goddard Blyth (2000) argues that more attention should be given to the development of motor skills when considering children's 'readiness' for the demands of formal schooling. She cites a range of practices and studies that are based on and/or demonstrate a link between motor abilities and school readiness, including readiness for literacy learning.

(Continued)

1. In the former Czechoslovakia, two tests were used to assess children's readiness for school (Westlake, 1997, personal communication to Goddard Blyth). These tests were designed to see whether or not a child could cross the midline, a skill essential for forming letters. The test included:

   - Whether or not a child could draw a circle in both a clockwise and anticlockwise direction.

   - Whether or not a child could touch their left ear with their right hand and their right foot with their left hand.

2. Goddard Blythe and Hyland (1998) found differences in the early development of a group of children aged seven to eight years who had reading, writing and copying difficulties, in comparison with a group of children without difficulties. They found a range of significant factors in the children's early development related to:

   - balance, motor skills and auditory processing;

   - the developmental stages of crawling commando-like on their tummies or creeping on hands and knees;

   - difficulty sitting still.

In addition, these children were:

- later learning to walk (over 16 months);

- later learning to talk, to ride a bicycle, catch a ball and carry out fine motor tasks such as doing up buttons and tying shoelaces.

Factors related to the development of phonological skills were also significant in this group:

- they were later at learning to talk;

- they had a history of more frequent ear, nose and throat infections in the first three years of life;

- they were hypersensitive or over-reactive to certain sounds at seven years of age.

These children did not grow out of their problems; rather, the discrepancy between the two groups increased with time as lack of early motor development continued to have an impact on cognitive skills that depend upon the motor system for their expression such as reading, writing and copying (Goddard Blythe, 2000, p156).

(Continued)

3. Goddard Blythe (2000, p156) notes that a common factor among many children with later learning difficulties was that none had passed through the developmental stages of crawling on their tummies or creeping on hands and knees. Crawling and creeping she argues represent the successful completion of several stages of motor development which assume that head control and independent use of upper and lower, left and right sections of the body have been established. While failure to crawl is not in itself a predictor of learning difficulties, Goddard Blythe (1995) notes that it is during the process of crawling and creeping that a child starts to synchronise balance, vision and proprioception, and to train hand–eye coordination at the same visual distance they will use to read and write some years later.

Clearly, our brains are highly adaptive and are able to shape themselves to the demands placed upon them, and, despite these arguments, children do adapt to the demands of schooling. However, there are significant differences between having to adapt and compensate rather than being developmentally ready to learn, and the evidence suggests that it can have an ongoing impact on children's learning (Johnson, 2014; Goddard Blythe, 2011, 2012; Pagini, 2012). One of the underpinning tenets of early years practice is that provision is distinctively different to school-based provision as it is developmentally appropriate for very young children. Johnson's (2014) analysis of our current approach to teaching reading is therefore significant in supporting our approach to teaching young children, enabling them to come to learning developmentally ready and so with a good chance of success. In terms of phonics, this means that children have a range of interconnected knowledge, skills and understandings before we embark on more formal aspects of phonics teaching: good spoken language; an awareness of the forms and functions of print; metalinguistic awareness; ability to symbolise; and good physical capabilities.

Providing for babies' and young children's physical development

To enable children to move through the necessary physical developmental pathways, and thus come to learning with a high chance of success, they need opportunities, and time and space to engage in appropriate physical activity, because physical capabilities emerge from physical movement. A professional understanding of the significant impact of physical activity on learning and what this means in terms of provision, is vital for early years practitioners (particularly as we are aware of children's decreasing levels of physical activity). The Physical Activity Statistics (BHF, 2015) reported that, overall in England, only 10 per cent of children aged 2–4 years met the recommended levels of activity, and recommended levels were achieved by only 21 per cent of boys and 16 per cent of girls age 5–15 years. These statistics marked a downward trend since 2008 in the number of children meeting the recommended levels of activity. So, if we are to accept that this is likely to have an impact on children's later learning, it is imperative that we in early years understand the importance of children developing good physical skills and provide well-focused and appropriate opportunities for them to do so.

Providing for babies' physical development to support learning

Physical development begins from birth, so babies need opportunities to develop and practise their emerging physical and sensory capabilities. Of particular significance are tummy time and crawling, opportunities for physical activity and movement such as standing, falling, spinning, rolling and being upside down, and rich sensory experiences.

Tummy time
Tummy time refers to the time babies spend in a prone position – lying on their tummy on the floor. O'Connor and Daly (2016, p52) identify the benefits of regular, supervised bursts of tummy time as:

* lengthening the spine and developing neck extensor muscles;

* expanding the chest cavity, allowing for deeper breathing;

* encouraging weight bearing through the hands, which is important in developing a full palm stretch, which in turn helps develop dexterity of the fingers and strength of grip;

* encouraging the eyes to focus and track at close range;

* helping to inhibit the early primitive reflexes (see Goddard Blyth (2010) above) – for example, those that tie head movement to the whole body (correct head alignment can only develop when the head is free to move separately);

* encouraging cross-lateral connections, which are important for higher level brain development;

* developing proprioception (*see* Johnson (2014) above);

* aiding awareness of bodily functions such as helping with toilet training.

Conversely, the problems associated with a lack of tummy time are:

* poor breath control leading to low energy;

* reduced weight bearing on the palms, causing difficulties with grasp and the later fine motor skills linked with pencil control and handwriting;

* visual and focusing problems likely to have an impact on later reading skills;

- poor bladder and bowel awareness and control;

- a lack of activity likely to inhibit early primitive reflexes, which can affect all aspects of physical development and body control.

However, despite known advantages of tummy time for babies, there is concern that many babies do not have sufficient tummy time. Reportedly (O'Connor and Daly, 2016), there are a number of factors that affect this.

- Changes in advice to parents that babies should be put to sleep on their backs rather than their fronts. This was in response to evidence on SIDS (sudden infant death syndrome, or 'cot-death'), and this has led to parents being more wary about putting babies on their tummies.

- Babies spending more time strapped into car seats, pushchairs and baby bouncers, and, with increased regulation about safety, these becoming increasingly more restrictive and children are required to be in them for a longer period of time.

- More children are in day-care, for more and longer days. This has inevitable time and space limitations, and there is a greater need for practitioners to understand the significance of tummy time.

Crawling

Crawling is essential for developing balance and coordination, proprioception and cross-laterality. Crawling builds muscle strength, balance and coordination as babies support their weight, and shift their weight from arms to legs and side to side. It supports proprioception as it enables babies to begin to get a sense of their body in space, and it patterns cross-lateral movement as legs and arms are working in rhythmic opposition to one another.

Babies need to be provided with the time and space to use and develop this physical capability, as Lamont (2001) observes, in addition to the benefits outlined above, crawling has many other benefits that lead into learning: *it influences the child's ability to focus, store and retrieve information, observe detail, coordinate right and left, and sequence.*

O'Connor and Daly (2016) support this, arguing that crawling is important for beginning to make connections between both sides of the brain, as it involves alternating intentional motor action. Crawling is also important because *the action helps to stabilise and co-ordinate both eyes together, improving depth perception and binocular focus, which will be very significant for later reading and writing* (O'Connor and Daly, 2016, p58).

Standing, falling, spinning, rolling and being upside down

Standing and falling are vital for children to find their balance and develop proprioceptive capabilities. Pulling themselves up and seeking for their balance to stand and eventually walk requires significant coordination of muscles and joints. Movement such as spinning, hanging upside down and rolling are also significant in children developing their vestibular and proprioceptive capabilities.

Sensory experiences

Babies need rich experiences that stimulate all their senses. Everything babies hear, see, taste, smell and touch strengthens connections in the brain. Therefore, it follows that the richer the experiences, the stronger the connections that can potentially be made. This does not mean assailing a baby with constant noisy and busy stimulus. Gentle experiences that stimulate the senses are effective, for example:

- skin-to-skin contact, holding, stroking and massaging;
- lying on a soft-textured blanket;
- quiet singing;
- eye contact while feeding and dressing;
- cupping and trickling warm water down their body in the bath;
- tummy time.

Providing for young children's physical development to support learning

Once children are standing and walking, they need to continue to develop and refine their physical capabilities including balance, coordination, proprioception, sensory integration and opportunities for activity that require that they cross their midline.

Balance and proprioceptive capabilities are developed and strengthened by children engaging in a range of large and small physical movement in which they experience pressure (Johnson, 2014). This includes all the obvious physical activities that involve bouncing, jumping, climbing, pushing and pulling, swinging and spinning. Activities that develop these skills are also part of everyday life and routinely provided in settings. Therefore, it is not necessary to do things differently, but to be aware that these early physical skills are vital in developing children's capacity to learn. Johnson (2014) lists examples of regular play- and home-based activities that are wonderful for developing and strengthening proprioceptive pathways: *digging ... , pushing a wheelbarrow, carrying shopping, pulling weeds, hanging from monkey bars and circle time games that involve clapping, stomping, hopping, galloping and skipping.*

In addition, children need opportunities for activity that involves cross-lateral movement to help to strengthen their bilateral integration pathways. Again, opportunities arise for this in everyday play activities and experiences; what is important is that the activity encourages children to reach, look or step across their midline. Some examples, among many, are:

- dancing;
- chasing and popping bubbles;
- den building;
- getting dressed and undressed, washing, cleaning teeth and brushing hair;

- sand and water play, where children are reaching across their body to fill containers with a scoop or spade;

- tidying up: sorting, stacking and boxing equipment;

- reading big books or using story boards that require children to scan from left to right;

- large-scale painting where children are making long movements that require them to reach across their body;

- using a torch in a den or wooded area to search for things;

- stirring or mixing: when cooking, mixing paint or in role-play activities;

- and, if you are adventurous, introducing movement activities based on martial arts – for example, tai chi or qigong, which involve a series of slow, gentle, repeated movements that build an awareness of the body in space and include movement that crosses the midline.

In addition, provision needs to be rich in activities that stimulate and engage children's senses that build on what they know and can do. They need opportunities to be active, to move to learn. They need the time, space and appropriate pedagogical interactions to enable them to explore and investigate, observe and imitate; to know, to respond, and to apply and integrate their knowledge.

Planning physical activities as literacy

When we are planning for children, it is important that what we plan is developmentally appropriate, which means that the activity is mapped to what the children need now and next. The advent of stated curricula for young children (Early Years Foundation Stage and the National Curriculum) risks a shift in our thinking so that we increasingly begin to think in the categories that are laid out for us, and we are drawn into using them as the starting point for our provision; thus, we become curriculum-focused rather than child-focused in both our thinking and provision. However, we know that children do not learn in discrete subject areas. Their learning is holistic and integrated, and far more complex and messy than a neat curriculum document suggests.

So, if we are to look beyond the curriculum and focus on what we know about the importance of physical skills to literacy learning, it can be argued that activities and experiences that support the development of balance, proprioception, cross-laterality and sensory awareness and integration *are* literacy. So, logically, alongside talking, books and engagement with print, they can be planned as literacy activities. In any stated curriculum, literacy will look like literacy and involve letters, sounds, paper and writing implements, but early literacy is also jumping, hopping, dancing, spinning, mixing, scanning, building, reaching, placing, filling and stacking. Therefore, if our provision is child-focused, this should be reflected in our planning and provision for early literacy, enabling children come to later, more formal literacy learning ready to learn and with a good chance of success.

Getting parents involved

In addition to an awareness of the health benefits of being active, it is important that we communicate to parents the additional benefits to children's learning: physical development is integral to learning, and children do not learn to sit still by sitting still. So, a trip to the park with a young child where they can run around, swing, spin, turn upside down, hang, balance, climb and crawl will help them to be able to sit still and focus, and it will support learning to read and write by developing strong links between the two sides of their brain. This could be communicated in all the usual ways through discussion at pick-up and drop-off, posters, leaflets, information evenings, parents' evenings and on social media and websites.

- Posters, leaflets, postcards, texts or emails (if permitted) with suggestions of easy ways to stimulate babies' senses in everyday routines and interactions.

- Instead of sending a book home over a weekend, suggest that parents take children to the park or play on a trampoline, have a go at skipping or go to a soft play area. All of this feeds into literacy, as does book reading.

- Teach children action rhymes that specifically encourage coordination and cross-lateral movement, and get the children to do them with their family.

- Encourage parents to teach you skipping/clapping games that they know, and have a go with the children.

- Make suggestions for TV programmes that encourage children to be actively involved.

- Be brave. When parents are concerned or children are struggling with demands of the EYFS, encourage parents to do more physical activity – move away from asking parents to try to make a child sit still and focus when they are not physically developmentally ready, and instead give parents the information to be able to support their child's physical capabilities that have been shown to lead into learning.

Conclusion

This chapter has looked at why physical development is integral to learning, including early literacy. It has identified balance, proprioception, crossing the midline and sensory awareness and integration as important physical capabilities that have an impact on brain development and learning, including children's ability to sit still and focus. Some physical activities that develop and nurture these necessary skills in babies and young children have been listed. The chapter has outlined why physical activities should be planned as literacy, and the importance of communicating this to parents and getting them involved in physical activities that lead into later literacy learning.

References

Archer, C and Siraj, I (2015) Measuring the quality of movement play in early childhood education settings: Linking movement-play and neuroscience. *European Early Childhood Research Journal*, 23(1): 21–42.

British Heart Foundation (BHF) (2015) Physical activity statistics. Available online at: **www.bhf.org.uk/publications/statistics/physical-activity-statistics-2015** (accessed 11 September 2016).

Connell, G and McCarthy, C (2014) *A Moving Child is a Learning Child*. Minneapolis, MN: Free Spirit Publishing.

Dolan, M (2000) Psycho-evolutionary strategies to teach reading. Available online at: **www.waece.org/biblioweb07/pdfs/d138.pdf** (accessed 11 September 2016).

Goddard Blythe, S (1995) In Goddard Blythe, S (2000) Early learning in the balance: Priming the first ABC. *Support for Learning*, 15(4): 154–8.

Goddard, Blyth, S and Hyland, D (1998) In Goddard Blythe, S (2000) Early learning in the balance: Priming the first ABC. *Support for Learning*, 15(4): 154–8.

Goddard Blythe, S (2000) Early learning in the balance: Priming the first ABC. *Support for Learning*, 15(4): 154–58.

Goddard Blythe, S (2011) Physical Foundations for Learning. In House, R (2011) *Too Much, Too Soon? Early Learning and the Erosion of Childhood*. Stroud: Hawthorne Press.

Goddard Blythe, S (2012) *Assessing Neuromotor Readiness for Learning*. London: Wiley-Blackwell.

Johnson, S (2014) A developmental approach looking at the relationship of children's foundational neurological pathways to their higher capacities for learning. Available at: **www.youandyourchildshealth.org/youandyourchildshealth/articles/teaching%20 our%20children.html** (accessed 11 September 2016).

Lamont, B (2001) Babies naturally. Available online at: **http://neurologicalreorganization.org/articles/babies-naturally/** (accessed 11 September 2016).

O'Connor, A and Daly, A (2016) *Understanding Physical Development in the Early Years. Linking Bodies and Minds*. London: Routledge.

Pagini, L (2012) Links between motor skills and indicators of school readiness at kindergarten entry in urban disadvantaged children. *Journal of Educational and Developmental Psychology*, 2(1): 95–107.

Reeves, MJ and Bailey, RP (2014) The effects of physical activity on children diagnosed with attention deficit hyperactivity disorder: A review. Education 3–13: *International Journal of Primary, Elementary and Early Years Education*, 1–13.

Sylva, K, Siraj Blatchford, I and Taggart, B (2006) In Archer, C and Siraj, I (2015) Measuring the quality of movement play in early childhood education settings: Linking movement-play and neuroscience. *European Early Childhood Research Journal*, 23(1): 21–42.

Whitebread, D and Bingham, S (2014) School Readiness: Starting Age, Cohorts and Transitions in the Early Years. In Moyles, J, Payler, J and Georgeson, J (2014) *Early Years Foundations: Critical Issues*. Maidenhead: Open University Press.

5   Metalinguistic development

Introduction

This chapter explains metalinguistic development as one aspect of metacognition. It outlines a model of children's metalinguistic development and discusses directionality in metalinguistic awareness. The chapter makes links between these skills and learning to read and write, and highlights the role of adults in achieving this. The benefits of being bilingual for children's metalinguistic awareness are outlined.

Developing the ability to think and talk about language are important aspects of what comes before phonics, and of phonics teaching. To be taught phonics effectively, children need to be able to think and talk about language. They need to understand that language can be talked about, and have a language to talk about it: this is called metalinguistic knowledge.

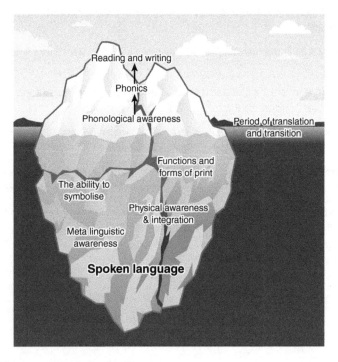

Figure 5.1   What comes before phonics

Metacognition and metalinguistics

As metalinguistic knowledge is an aspect of metacognition, metacognition is outlined in the chapter to provide the wider context for metalinguistics. It is only covered briefly and there is a significant body of work that much more fully explores children's cognition and metacognition. What this highlights is the holistic nature of learning: that language and cognition are inextricably linked. We separate children's learning and development into areas and topics to aid our understanding (and to write about it), whereas children's actual learning is integrated and interdependent.

Both metacognition and metalinguistic knowledge are skills that we develop and use throughout life. Therefore, when discussing these skills in relation to young children, we are referring to their emerging abilities to think about thinking and language, and their use of language to describe these processes.

The terms used in the field of metalinguistics are often unclear (Bialystok, 2001), therefore for clarity two terms are used in the chapter: metalinguistic awareness to refer to the early stages of children becoming aware of language; and metalinguistic knowledge to refer to later stages when children have developed explicit representations of aspects of linguistic structures (Bialystok, 2001).

What is metalinguistic awareness and knowledge?

Metalinguistic knowledge is an aspect of metacognition. It is the ability to think and talk about language.

Initially, children learn and use language in functional ways – to communicate with others, to get things that they want and to manage others. Language in these instances is used in an implicit, unanalysed way. Metalinguistic awareness is children's growing ability to 'see' language beyond this functional use; to switch attention from the functional use of language and focus on the language itself. It requires that children learn to think about, and manipulate, the structural features of language (Lightsey and Frye, 2004). Metalinguistic development is part of children's broader metacognitive development.

Metacognition

Metacognition refers to our ability to be aware of and regulate our own thinking. This skill is an integral part of learning effectively. When we are learning we need to be able to monitor and regulate our mental processes and draw on cognitive strategies to help us. For example, when reading a book we quickly become aware of whether or not we have understood the text. This shows that we are monitoring our mental processes as we read. We can then reflect on our thinking and talk about it at many levels: whether we have understood the text or not; what we have understood; what we haven't understood; why we have or have not understood aspects of the text. We can then control our cognitive processes. So, if we have understood the text we would perhaps carry on in the same way; if not, we might reread more slowly and precisely, we might read out loud, or we might actively think about or discuss what we have read. So an important part of reading and understanding this text effectively is our ability to monitor, reflect on, control and regulate our cognitive processes. Language is integral to this ability: we use language to monitor, reflect, control and communicate these cognitive processes.

Young children need to develop metacognition. They need to become aware of their mental processes and then, as they grow and learn, to strengthen and deepen their ability to become aware of cognitive strategies and use them effectively. This ability is important when learning to read and write, including learning phonics. Children need to be aware of, and monitor and regulate their responses to words and text – for example, what they understand about phonics, vocabulary, grammar, text structure, text cohesion or inference.

Brown's (1987, in Whitebread, 2010) interrelated elements of metacognition are a useful way to understand different aspects of metacognition.

- Metacognitive experience: monitoring and self-awareness of mental processes and reflections on it.

- Metacognitive knowledge: knowledge gained from metacognitive experience, about our own mental processing, including the cognitive strategies that we employ.

- Metacognitive control: the appropriate use of mental strategies that we have developed, based on our metacognitive experience and knowledge.

For young children to begin to develop metacognition they need opportunities and encouragement to think about thinking. Thinking is a silent, internal process. It becomes evident when we reveal it through what we do, or what we say. The way in which we interact with children is therefore very important. We need to provide these opportunities for them to become aware of their thinking and, in time, to be aware of the strategies that they are using and to communicate this to us. This perhaps sounds more complex than it is. We can do this in our daily interactions with young children, as in the following examples.

- As you begin an activity ask the children to think about what you did last time, why you did it, what you used and why, and what happened.

- Commenting on children's activity by referring to their thinking – for example: 'I can see that you have thought really carefully about the colours that you have used in your painting and used black and white for the penguins, just like the ones in the book that we read yesterday.'

- Revealing your thinking, as a model of cognitive processes, as you complete a task. For example: when packing large outdoor equipment into a shed you can think out loud; ponder what needs to go in first, which order things need to go in, note when items don't fit and the changes that you will make to fit it all in.

In these ways, thinking, which is usually a silent internal process, is evident to the children and they can begin to get a sense of cognitive processes at work and the language that we use to refer to these processes.

Metalinguistic awareness and knowledge

An important aspect of metacognition is metalinguistic knowledge: the ability to think and talk about language. Metalinguistic knowledge is the ability to treat language as an object composed of words and meanings. It is the ability to recognise that language has a structure, that it consists of words, that words have meaning, and that the structure of language – the words and meanings – can be examined, discussed and manipulated. Metalinguistic knowledge begins as children start to become aware of language beyond its functional use, and 'see' language. Lightley and Frye (2004, p35) describe it as follows:

> Downing (1979) likens language to a glass through which children view the world (in Snow, et al., 1998, p. 45). At first they do not suspect that it has its own existence or aspects of construction, yet in order to grow in literacy this perception must change. Children must treat language as an object of thought. They must develop metalinguistic awareness or the ability to think about and play with language apart from its meaning.

The link between this and phonics is clear: learning phonics requires that children can treat language as something to be analysed. It requires that they have an understanding that language has a structure with rules and patterns that govern it, and that we can learn and manipulate these rules and patterns to create words and meaning. This early meta-awareness of language is vital in supporting children's later phonics learning, as Keith (1997, p12) argues, *terminology and rules are pointless if your mind hasn't grasped the concepts behind the terminology*. Thus, in terms of what comes before phonics, children need opportunities that trigger their awareness of language as an object, and continued experience and appropriate opportunities to enable this early awareness to become increasingly more explicit. As children then move into learning phonics and become readers and writers, this metalinguistic knowledge about the structure and properties of language (Brooks and Kempe, 2012) will enable them to develop and use explicit strategies to shape, monitor and reflect on their reading and writing.

A model of metalinguistic development

Gombert (1992) provides a four-phase model for the development of children's metalinguistic knowledge. Although some aspects of his model have been critiqued, it remains the most comprehensive consideration of metalinguistic knowledge (Myhill *et al.*, 2012).

Gombert's model of metalinguistic development

Phase 1. The acquisition of first linguistic skills

Children acquire and consolidate early language. This occurs in a child's family and community and is triggered by modelling and feedback from others. In this phase language use is implicit and unanalysed.

The next phase is triggered as children's language use becomes more sophisticated and the communication demands from others progressively greater. Children are therefore required to resolve these increasingly complex demands of communication.

Phase 2. The acquisition of epi-linguistic control

In this phase children organise the implicit language ability acquired in the initial phase. This results in greater functional control of language. This is evident in the application of language rules which become increasingly general in scope and progressively constitute a system. For example, ungrammatical utterances are shaped to become grammatically correct. This is acquired as a result of the enrichment of the models and feedback from others.

Gombert (1992, p190) argues that epi-linguistic control is essential, as *only that which has already been mastered at a functional level can be so at a conscious level*. Once epi-linguistic control is stable and effective in the management of everyday verbal exchanges, new, fresh stimulus is required to move towards metalinguistic knowledge.

Phase 3. The acquisition of metalinguistic knowledge

In this phase children become consciously aware of aspects of language: knowledge about language (declarative knowledge) and knowledge about how to use language (procedural knowledge). This conscious knowledge arises from expectations and demands placed on the child that act as triggers. For example, reading and writing necessitate conscious knowledge and intentional control of numerous aspects of language, so opportunities for children to engage with books and print triggers the need for declarative and procedural knowledge and mediated engagement develops this. This relationship is therefore bidirectional: early metalinguistic development facilitates the acquisition of abilities, which, being necessary to this knowledge, then stimulate it in their turn (Gombert, 1992, p190).

Importantly, Gombert (1992, p191) notes that *declarative metalinguistic knowledge precedes metalinguistic control and the application of this knowledge*. Knowledge about language comes before the ability to consciously apply this knowledge – there is a developmental hierarchy (Myhill *et al.*, 2012). Gombert (1992) also notes that the move into metalinguistic knowledge is non-obligatory. He concludes that the triggers to move children's understanding forward must occur for metalinguistic knowledge to develop.

Phase 4. The automation of the processes

In this phase the meta-processes become automated – i.e. they are not consciously controlled. However, meta-processes are readily available to the conscious mind when required. Thus, if an obstacle impairs the automatic function of a linguistic process, the automated process can be replaced with meta-processes – for example, our use of grammatically correct language becomes automated until we misuse or don't know a word, then we need to consciously draw on meta-processes to think about the language that we are using.

Age and phases

Gombert (1992, p191) makes some observations about the age of access, arguing that it is about six to seven years of age that the first meta-functions are generally identifiable, so the *first stable epi-linguistic controls do not appear before the end of the fifth year*. Similarly, Karmiloff-Smith *et al.* (1994) in their study looked at children's understanding of a 'word' and concluded that it was between the ages of 4½–5 years old that children were able to differentiate between 'word' and 'thing.'

DEVELOP YOUR UNDERSTANDING

Make sure that you understand Gombert's model of metalinguistic development.

Gombert argues that meta-functions are generally identifiable about age six to seven years, and stable epi-linguistic control at the end of the fifth year.

Karmiloff-Smith *et al.* (1994) explored the notion of children's understanding of a word. In their study, children listened to a story in which the narrator paused and asked the children to repeat 'the last word' or 'the last thing' that she had said. Their results showed that children aged 4½–5 years old were able to differentiate between 'word' and 'thing'.

- Consider Gombert and Karmiloff Smith *et al.*'s conclusions alongside language and literacy curriculum and assessment requirements in the Early Years Foundation Stage and the National Curriculum for KS1.

  o How does their work challenge the requirements of these curricula?

  o What are the implications of this for phonics teaching and learning?

There are a number of highly relevant points from Gombert's model in relation to what comes before phonics. His work confirms and enhances much of what we know about early experiences that enable children to become literate.

- The acquisition of spoken language is the basis of metalinguistic knowledge.

- Knowledge of language comes before being able to control and manipulate it.

- Becoming literate requires a cognitive shift from implicit to explicit knowledge.

- Development of metalinguistic knowledge necessitates mediation – it doesn't happen of its own accord.

- Other people in a child's world are vital in facilitating metalinguistic knowledge.

- The relationship is bi-directional – having metalinguistic knowledge facilitates further development of metalinguistic knowledge. This has resonances with the Matthew effect of reading (*see* Chapter 2).

- With age, appropriate opportunities to learn and consolidate their learning, children's meta-processes become automated. This has a positive effect: children's meta-processes are automated so they are able to focus on other aspects of learning, whilst also having the capacity to consciously analyse language when needed.

Directionality

Directionality refers to the ways in which learning impacts on other learning. The question about metalinguistic knowledge is whether we develop metalinguistic knowledge then apply it, or develop metalinguistic knowledge by using metalinguistic strategies. For example, with regard to phonics teaching, do children need phonemic awareness (the ability to hear and discriminate between sounds) to learn phonic sounds, or do children learn to hear and discriminate between sounds by learning phonic sounds? Phonemic awareness (an important metalinguistic skill) will be considered in more detail in Chapter 7 but, as a general point, this question of directionality is an important consideration when thinking about the pedagogy of early literacy, including phonics.

Developing metalinguistic knowledge and control is generally regarded as bidirectional: both processes have an impact on one another. We develop metalinguistic knowledge then apply it, and metalinguistic knowledge is supported and developed by using metalinguistic strategies. As Gombert (1992) argues, early metalinguistic awareness seems to facilitate the acquisition of abilities, so children who are already able to analyse language consciously (declarative knowledge) can devote their focus and energies to learning the rules of use (procedural knowledge).

Pedagogically, Gombert's model highlights the necessity of actively supporting children's early language and metalinguistic development. The effect of this is twofold: to trigger later metalinguistic knowledge that is essential to becoming literate, and to provide opportunities for children to use their emerging awareness and knowledge to support further development.

Supporting children's metalinguistic knowledge

Metalinguistic awareness and knowledge require that children objectify language; they see it as something that we can analyse independently from its meaning and function. Initially, children will use language functionally, as a tool for communication and meeting their needs, so they need to learn to see language as something that they can reflect on, analyse, talk about and manipulate. Teachers and practitioners who work with young children therefore need to provide opportunities to enable them to become aware of aspects of language and then to use this knowledge as they move into becoming literate. This can be achieved in a number of ways including, through interaction, the use of story books and language play.

Interaction

First and foremost, we need to focus on children's spoken language. As with all aspects of literacy, spoken language is the basis of metalinguistic awareness and knowledge. Therefore, a strong focus on supporting children's language acquisition and development is essential. As Gombert (1992, p190) notes, functional control of language is essential as *only that which has already been mastered at a functional level can be so at a conscious level.*

In addition to supporting children's more general spoken language, our interaction needs to have particular features to enable children to become consciously aware of language, and to trigger and develop metalinguistic awareness and knowledge.

- We need to use the language for language, and draw children's attention to language in concrete and meaningful ways in our interactions in adult-led and child-initiated play. For example, when encouraging children to share resources, we can draw children's attention to language as we model appropriate language use: 'If you want the big bricks don't just take them, use language, say, "please can I have the big bricks?" and they will pass them to you.'

- We also need to draw children's attention to the details of language in our inter-actions: to the particular words that we use; the ways in which we use them; the rules that govern them; the constituent parts of words (phonemes, graphemes); and how we build up and break down words to read (segment and blend). This can be achieved in everyday interactions, as the following examples.

  o Draw children's attention to language and actively highlight features of the language. Point out the words on children's clothing, read the words to them, segment and blend them as a model of decoding, discuss why particular words have been chosen. Is it to name the character, a brand, a slogan, a statement? Discuss which other words could have been used. Talk about words on other clothing that you have seen them in. Similarly, if using a visual timetable to pattern the day, use words with the photographs and symbols, and each day draw children's attention to the words. Point out that different words are chosen each day because they map the pictures and activities available that day. Perhaps use humour by putting incorrect words with pictures and getting children to help you match the correct word with the picture or symbol – the use of misunderstanding is a good pedagogical strategy to get children to think actively about words.

  o When writing a child's name, articulate the phonemes and tell the child that these sounds make up their name. Tell them that this word says their name. Look together at the graphemes used in the child's name, talk about where else they have seen the letters. Develop this by writing a child's first and family name. Use the same interaction when modelling writing in all other situations.

This pattern of using commentary and discussion to alert children to the features of language can be used across the provision. What it requires is that that staff (and parents) are consciously aware of doing it each time the opportunity arises. These moments are often referred to as 'teachable moments' – a situation in which the opportunity to teach something arises in a meaningful context. In this way, young children have the opportunities to develop metalinguistic awareness in their play and everyday interactions at home and in settings.

Olsen's (1988) work, outlined below, supports the importance of interaction in developing children's metalinguistic awareness and knowledge. He argues that these patterns of interaction are embedded in some children's early language acquisition at home, and this has a positive impact on their metalinguistic awareness and knowledge and, in turn, their later literacy learning.

See! Jumping! Some oral language antecedents of literacy (Olsen, 1988)

Olsen's argument is that the *roots of literacy lie in how we learn to talk* (Olsen, 1988, p226). He notes that literate parents make the assumption that language is something that needs to be taught through interaction and literacy-based experiences and activities. In addition, he argues, that literate parents transmit a literate orientation in the process of teaching their children to talk. His hypothesis is that, as these children learn to talk they also learn a set of concepts for referring to language.

He concludes by claiming that his work slightly alters the existing view: that antecedents of literacy lie in language capability, and that children from more literate homes have a larger vocabulary than those from less literate homes because they are exposed to larger vocabularies. It alters it, Olsen (1988) argues, in claiming that because of the nature of the interaction in literate homes, in addition to exposure to rich language these children also have

> *important and relevant parts of their vocabulary that pertain to the structure and meaning of language – the metalanguage – and to mental states implicated by the metalanguage.*

And this is

> *applied to oral language by literate parents and taught to their children as part of ordinary speech.*

> (Olsen, 1988, p229)

Olsen (1988) offers the example of a parent teaching the word 'jumping' as an explication of this process. He notes that a common practice among literate parents is the use of picture books to teach children nouns, so pictures are pointed out and if the child doesn't know what it is, the parent names it. Olsen (1988) argues that this same process can be observed when teaching other parts of speech, such as verbs. The example is given of a mother pointing to a frog jumping and saying 'See! Jumping!' – the action is lifted from the context and taught explicitly. Olsen (1988) suggests that such parents are teaching children to talk in a manner appropriated from the practice of teaching them to read: teaching the child not just how to use words but also the structure of language as an object composed of words and meanings. In addition, he cites supporting evidence that children who learn to speak in more literate homes have been shown to ask more questions about language – the meanings of words and phrases. He concludes that this demonstrates that

> *Like their literate parents such children come to recognise (or believe) that language has a structure, that it consists of words, that words have meaning and that these structures can be discussed by use of a metalanguage.*

> (Olsen, 1988, p225)

Story books

Reading and discussing story and picture books supports children's metalinguistic awareness and knowledge. Reading books draws children's attention to words and language at many levels. An early example of this is children's patterning of favourite texts that enables them to anticipate the language and storyline, and tell you if you miss or change words or the story. This marks the beginning of an awareness of the language, beginning to 'see' that words exist beyond their meaning.

Discussion of aspects of the books enhances this early awareness. For example, in discussion about the language you may focus on the meaning of the words, why a particular word has been chosen, whether words could be used instead to keep the meaning or to change the meaning of the sentence, rhyming, alliterative or onomato-poeic words. For example, in *Alfie Gets in First* (Hughes, 2009), the little boy Alfie cries when he locks himself inside the house and his mum is outside. Discussion of different words to describe how Alfie feels will draw children's attention to language, including the fact that there are *words* and that they have meanings, and we can choose which *word* we use. This discussion will also naturally include the language for language: the adult will talk about the word 'upset', and other words with the same meaning that could replace it. These small, everyday interactions build and develop young children's awareness of language: that we can talk about, use, make choices and manipulate language, which are all important beginnings in developing metalinguistic knowledge.

Language play

Playing with language in the form of poems, rhymes, nonsense words and stories, riddles, jokes, puns, puzzles, and alliterative and onomatopoeic language is an excellent way to alert children to language: that it has a structure, that it consists of words and that words have meaning, and that these words and meanings can be analysed and discussed (Olsen, 1988). Crystal (1998) describes language play as the bending and breaking of linguistic rules, and it is the awareness that comes from this engagement that alerts children to structure and meaning in language which, in turn, supports metalinguistic awareness and knowledge, and leads to early literacy, including phonics.

Zipke (2008) addresses the role of riddles and jokes more specifically. He argues that riddles and jokes are highly enjoyable ways to develop metalinguistic awareness, in that the humour in riddles and jokes stimulates and enhances metalinguistic skill by requiring children to understand multiple meanings of words, metaphors and idioms, detect ambiguity in words and to understand perceptual shifts. He outlines a range of ways to use riddles in a setting or classroom.

- Have riddle and joke books on the bookshelf for children to choose.
- Read riddles and jokes to the children at group times – make sure that you explain how language was manipulated in the riddle to make them laugh. It is not unusual for children to laugh at jokes and riddles because they think that is what they should do, rather than having understood the word play.

- Encourage children to make up riddles and jokes. You should notice how these progress as children become increasingly sensitive to language play.

- Get children to tell jokes and riddles. Think aloud and explain clearly the ambiguity contained within it.

- Make connections as you read other texts – highlight and comment on ambiguous language as you read to children. Think aloud about the ambiguities in the language.

This pattern of interaction and language play that enables children to use and manipulate language are confirmed in Myhill *et al.*'s (2012) study outlined below.

WHAT DOES RESEARCH TELL US?

Rethinking grammar: the impact of embedded grammar teaching on students' writing and students' metalinguistic understanding (Myhill et al. 2012)

In their study, Myhill *et al.* (2012) outline a series of underpinning pedagogical principles that concur with the ways of supporting children's metalinguistic development outlined above. These include the following examples.

- Meta-language should be used but always explained through examples.
- A positive pedagogical strategy is the use of imitation: offering models for children to play with and use.
- Inclusion of activities that encourage talking about language and effects.
- The use of authentic examples from authentic texts.
- The use of activities which support children in making choices.
- The encouragement of language play, experimentation and games.

  In addition, with reference to pedagogy of metalinguistic awareness, they concluded that teacher's mediation of metalinguistic knowledge was significant, in particular *an ability to define and explain metalinguistic terminology appropriately.*

  (Myhill *et al.*, 2012, p162)

Clearly, in addition to their awareness of the structure and meaning in language, children's developing awareness of language and how it works is inextricably linked to language comprehension. As children become able to reflect on language and talk about structure and meaning, their ability to understand and respond to all aspects of texts is enhanced. The Simple View of Reading (*see* Chapter 1) outlines that reading is a combination of decoding and comprehension. Therefore, the development of good metalinguistic knowledge supports both these aspects of reading. Writing also requires the ability to analyse and manipulate meaning and structure in language, so, again, good early metalinguistic knowledge is important in its anticipation of later literacy development.

Metalinguistic knowledge and comprehension

Oakhill *et al.* (2015), identify the two essential aspects of effective reading as word reading and language comprehension. This is in line with the simple view of reading (*see* Chapter 1). Phonics, the main subject of this book, enables word reading, and language comprehension enables the text to be understood. Language comprehension, they argue, requires that, as we read, we build a mental model of the text that is an overall representation of the meaning. This requires a range of processes and skills, many of which draw on metalinguistic (and metacognitive) knowledge. They identify five components in language comprehension that come together to enable us to comprehend what we read.

- Activating word meanings: knowing the meaning of words; knowing the meaning of words in context; monitoring which words we know and those that we don't.

- Understanding sentences: word order, syntactic construction, links in meaning across sentences (text coherence), including sentence connectives that can significantly change meaning.

- Making inferences: the use of background and additional knowledge to support meaning in the text.

- Comprehension monitoring: keeping track of whether the text makes sense, and making attempts to work out and remedy things if not.

- Understanding text structure: an understanding of the structure of different text genres – for example, narrative, non-fiction, email, newspaper article, book index.

They conclude that *successful comprehension involves the construction of a clear, complete and integrated mental representation of the meaning of a text: a mental model* (Oakhill *et al.*, 2015, p105). Building this mental model requires that children have metalinguistic knowledge: knowledge about the structure and properties of language (Brooks and Kempe, 2012). Zipke's (2008) study outlined below confirms this. His study highlights the importance of metalinguistic knowledge in language comprehension.

WHAT DOES RESEARCH TELL US?

Teaching metalinguistic awareness and reading comprehension with riddles (Zipke, 2008)

Zipke's (2008) paper focuses on word play, the ability to manipulate language which is both fun for children and enables them to make discoveries about language. These discoveries, he argues, support the metalinguistic knowledge necessary for reading.

As background to the study, he highlights the importance of understanding ambiguity in language to text comprehension. He argues that understanding that words and sentences can have more than one meaning improves comprehension by allowing readers to think flexibly about what the appropriate meaning may be. Additionally, that to evaluate and

(Continued)

WHAT DOES RESEARCH TELL US? *continued*

regulate comprehension of text, it is necessary to know that the words in a text can add up to more than one possible meaning. This ability to reflect upon and manipulate language is crucial for reading. Zipke (2008) gives a number of illustrative examples that have been used with children to elicit their understanding of ambiguity in language.

- The child talked about the problem with the teacher.
- The man's nails were very sharp.
- Kids make nutritious snacks.
- Homonyms such as 'can' – the ability to do something, and a metal receptacle.

Zipke (2008) conducted two studies to explore this relationship.

The first study looked at the correlation between the metalinguistic awareness and reading comprehension of children who were established readers. He assessed the ability of 100 children and found, as expected, that *the ability to recognise sentences with two meanings and the ability to solve riddles with lexical or syntactical ambiguity correlated significantly with reading comprehension* (Zipke, 2008, p130).

Zipke (2008) then conducted a follow-up study to explore this correlation between metalinguistic awareness and reading comprehension. A total of 46 third-graders (8-year-olds) from low socio-economic backgrounds were separated into two groups. Half the children were a control group who, once a week, read and discussed a book with the researcher. Half who received training sessions focused on words and sentences with multiple meanings: practice in identifying and defining homonyms; identifying and defining different types of ambiguous sentences; reading and writing riddles with lexical and structural riddles.

He found that the students who received metalinguistic training improved significantly more from pre-test to post-test than the control group on a comprehension monitoring assessment.

Zipke (2008) argues that these studies support the hypothesis that metalinguistic awareness supports reading comprehension. In addition, using riddles meant that the children enjoyed the sessions and responded enthusiastically. Using riddles to support metalinguistic awareness, he argues, has rich potential.

Metalinguistic knowledge and bilingualism

The awareness that language has a structure, that it consists of words that have meaning, and that these words and meanings are chosen and can be discussed is an integral feature of the linguistic landscape of children who are living in two or more languages. Bilingualism reveals aspects of language because children who move between languages are required to understand and use different words for the same thing, and different language structures to communicate and express meaning. This code-switching between languages has been shown to enhance an awareness of aspects of the structure and properties of a language. Bialystok (1986, 1988) explored this in studies designed to test why bilingual children showed this advantage. In one study she asked children to make judgements about whether a sentence was said 'the right way' or 'the wrong way'. Brooks and Kempe (2012, p183) describe the study thus:

> A semantically plausible sentence like 'Apples growed on trees' required children to ignore the meaningfulness of the sentence to identify the grammatical error (growed should be grew), whereas a semantically implausible sentence like 'Apples grow on noses' required children to ignore the implausible meaning of the sentence to identify the sentence as grammatically correct.

Bialystok found that bilingual children performed better at this task, and suggested that this was because they were more able to suppress irrelevant semantic information when judging the sentences. Further studies have explored and developed Bialystok's conclusion and found similarly, that bilingual children show improved metalinguistic awareness in contrast to their monolingual peers (Brooks and Kempe, 2012). Interestingly, other studies have shown that advantages associated with being bilingual may arise even before children have started to speak: that it is sufficient for young infants to process two languages to reap some benefits, as *exposure to two languages from birth enhances cognitive control of attention right from the start* (Brooks and Kempe, 2012, p185).

Conclusion

This chapter has looked at metalinguistic awareness and knowledge as one aspect of metacognition. It has briefly described and discussed metacognition, noting that children's cognition is a significant field of enquiry in itself, and recognising that children's learning is integrated and interdependent. Metalinguistic awareness and knowledge are defined and Gombert's (1992) model of metalinguistic development is outlined. Links to previously discussed aspects of children's literacy learning are made, and the relationship between metalinguistic development and phonics learning described. Ways in which practitioners and teachers can support metalinguistic development are considered, including the importance of specific types of interaction, use of story books and language play. The importance of metalinguistic development to language comprehension, as well as word reading, is acknowledged, and aspects of language comprehension that involve metalinguistic knowledge are described. How bilingualism enhances early metalinguistic awareness and knowledge is outlined.

References

Bialystok, E (1986, 1988) In Brooks, PJ, Kempe, V (2012) *Language Development*. Chichester: BPS Blackwell.

Bialystok, E (2001) *Bilingualism in Development: Language, Literacy and Cognition*. Cambridge: Cambridge University Press.

Brooks, PJ and Kempe, V (2012) *Language Development*. Chichester: BPS Blackwell.

Crystal, D (1998) *Language Play*. London: Penguin Books.

Gombert, JE (1992) *Metalinguistic Development*. Chicago: Chicago Press.

Hughes, S (2009) *Alfie Gets in First*. London: Red Fox Picture Books.

Karmiloff-Smith, A, Grant, J, Sims, K, Jones, MC and Cuckle, P (1994) Rethinking metalinguistic awareness: Representing and accessing knowledge about what counts as a word. *Cognition* (58)2: 197–219.

Keith, G (1997) In Myhill, D, Jones, S, Lines, H, Watson, A (2012) Re-thinking grammar: The impact of embedded grammar teaching on student's writing and student's metalinguistic understanding. *Research Papers in Education*, 27(2): 139–66.

Lightsey, B and Frye, J (2004) Teaching metalinguistic skills to enhance early reading instruction. *Reading Horizons* 45(1): 28–37 Available online at: **http://scholarworks.wmich.edu/cgi/viewcontent.cgi?article=1158&context=reading_horizons** (accessed 11 September 2016).

Myhill, D, Jones, S, Lines, H and Watson, A (2012) Re-thinking grammar: The impact of embedded grammar teaching on student's writing and student's metalinguistic understanding. *Research Papers in Education*, 27(2): 139–66.

Oakhill, J, Cain, K and Elbro, C (2015) *Understanding and Teaching Reading Comprehension: A Handbook*. London: Routledge.

Olsen, DR (1988) See! Jumping! Some oral language antecedents of literacy. In Mercer, N (1988) (ed.) *Language and Literacy from an Educational Perspective*. Berkshire: Oxford University Press.

Whitebread, D (2010) Play metacognition and self-regulation. In Broadhead, P, Howard, J, and Wood, E (2010) (eds) *Play and Learning in the Early Years*. London: SAGE.

Zipke, M (2008) Teaching metalinguistic awareness and reading comprehension with riddles. *The Reading Teacher*, 62(2): 128–37.

6 Print awareness

Introduction

Developing print awareness is an important aspect of what comes before phonics. Engagement with print in their everyday lives enables children to develop an understanding of why, where and how print is used. Becoming aware of the contexts where reading and writing are used draws children's attention to the need to be able to read and write and thus places learning phonics in a meaningful context.

This chapter considers what is meant by print awareness and what children need to understand about the functions and forms of print, including digital print. It looks at how children learn about this in a meaningful way at home and in settings, and how this supports children's move into learning phonics. It considers this issue for children who are bilingual, and discusses involving parents in engaging their children with print.

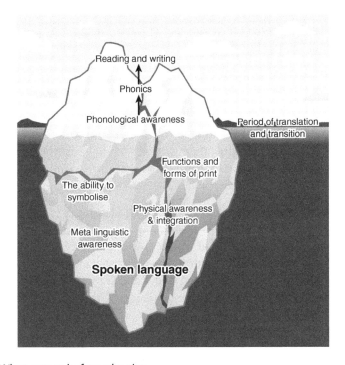

Figure 6.1   What comes before phonics

Roots of literacy

'Roots of literacy' is a metaphor used by Yetta Goodman (1986). Goodman suggests that as we observe children, we can see them inventing, discovering and developing understandings about literacy as they grow up in a literate environment. Her work on early literacy also concludes that children are alive to literacy and developing skills and concepts long before they become conventionally literate. As Ashton observes:

> *Undoubtedly the most critical period for the development of the skills and behaviours that influence effective language and literacy outcomes in later years encompasses the child's first year and continues through to the time they are ready for school ... the more formal expressions of literacy promoted in the years following school entry should be merely an end point in what is a continuum of learning about literacy, which begins at birth.*

(Ashton, 2013, p131)

Goodman (1986) argues that the beginnings of literacy occur as children become aware and begin to realise that written language makes sense and simultaneously begin to wonder *how* it makes sense. It is this exploration of the literate environment that enables children to develop their 'roots of literacy'. These roots include the following.

- Print awareness in situational contexts: children become aware that print carries meaning as they see it used in day-to-day situations such as on packaging, signs and logos.

- Print awareness in connected discourse: children become aware of the print in written material such as books, magazines, newspapers, letters.

- Functions and forms of writing: children become aware of the many ways in which we use print in our day-to-day lives; they begin to notice how we write and read, and that reading and writing are different.

- Oral language about written language: children begin to talk about reading and writing, which reflects their growing awareness of the uses of reading and writing in a literate society. They begin to learn words that refer to language, such as letter or word (*see* Chapter 5).

- Metalinguistic and metacognitive awareness (*see* Chapter 5).

Goodman continues her metaphor of 'roots' in her observation that children need the fertile soil of a literate environment in which to grow and learn. In this way, early literacy will emerge as children seek out and explore literacy practices. The knowledge and skill that arises from this early engagement with print is often referred to as 'emergent reading and writing'.

Print awareness

Print awareness refers to children's engagement with, and developing awareness of print in their environment and its use in the day-to-day life of their family and community.

Print awareness at this stage is about coming to know what print is, what it is used for and broadly how it works. This is often referred to as the 'functions' and 'forms' of print. An understanding of these functions and forms is important for later emergent literacy practices and phonics learning as it provides the context for learning to read and write. Young children's engagement with print enables them to come to know why, and where reading and writing are used, so emergent literacy in play and later more formal learning is set in a meaningful context. Children's earliest engagement with print is likely to be in the form of environmental print, story books and increasingly in the digital environment.

Environmental print

Environmental print is the print that children are surrounded by in their daily lives. It is often a combination of words, colours and images, and can be found across all aspects of their daily lives: on packaging; as advertising; on household appliances and controls; as print on clothing, on labels, branding or captions; through digital technology on phones, computers and other hand-held devices; as shop signs and logos. This print becomes meaningful to the child as they see and use it in meaningful ways in their everyday lives.

However, this does not necessarily mean that children can read the print: they can recognise it and know that it carries a particular meaning, but they are heavily dependent on the context of the print. Goodall (1994) found that children can recognise words when they are in their usual context – for example, a slogan on a particular item of clothing or the name of a product on a package, but are not able to read the word without these contextual clues. This is to be expected at an early stage. The important conceptual development is that print carries meaning and by reading the print we can understand that meaning. Additionally, environmental print can stimulate questions and discussion about reading: about why we read; about how we read; about letters and sounds; and about meanings of words, print and reading.

The importance of this early engagement with environmental print is supported by Neumann *et al.* (2011) in the study below. Their study reviewed the research evidence on the role of environmental print in children's emergent literacy, concluding that it has an important place in children's early literacy development.

WHAT DOES RESEARCH TELL US?

The role of environmental print in emergent literacy (Neumann et al., 2011)

Neumann *et al.* undertook a review of the evidence about *whether environmental print has value as a literary learning resource and, if so, the mechanisms by which it promotes literacy development* (Neumann et al., 2011, p231). They defined environmental print as surrounding, non-continuous print, encountered in a particular context which fulfils

(Continued)

---

real-life functions. It differs from the continuous print found in books and magazines. It is often visually attractive and personally meaningful to the child – for example, house-hold and environmental logos, branding and signs. Through sociocultural experiences with environmental print, young children fulfil real-life functions – for example, a specific label on a box means that it contains their favourite food.

The study recognised that there are two potential ways in which environmental print may influence literacy development.

1. A resource for children as they independently explore their environment.

2. A resource that parents, practitioners and teachers can use to promote early literacy skills.

They also note that children's experiences with environmental print are embedded within a sociocultural context and are dependent upon visual skills starting from birth.

Their wide-ranging review of research evidence showed that many children have a natural attraction to environmental print – for example, on food packaging and signs and logos, and that parents and early childhood educators should capitalise on this to promote children's literacy development. Their review of evidence suggests that environmental print can play an important role in literacy development. Interaction with environmental print in a child's sociocultural context will develop their logographic reading skills, which in turn will promote emergent literacy skills and conventional reading skills. Mediation of print in the environment by parents and teachers will encourage children's natural exploration of print in their world.

Neumann *et al.* (2011) conclude that

> *using environmental print scaffolding to foster children's already existing knowledge of print awareness and letter knowledge, and their print motivation, could benefit children prior to attending school, as well as potentially benefiting reading development after commencing school.'*

(Neumann *et al.*, 2011, p253)

Books

Engagement with books is the other vital aspect of children's earliest engagement with print. Reading books to children contributes to their awareness of print. However, before we consider the ways in which books can support children's awareness of print it is important to think about the role of books and stories in our lives. Stories enrich all our lives. Think about social situations when you weave a story to your friends, how enjoyable both the telling and the hearing of stories is in this situation. Think about social media, how we tell the story of ourselves. Think about how we engage with powerful stories in books, films, songs, theatre and dance. This love of stories begins in children's earliest years and storybooks are an important aspect of this. So, first and foremost we need to read books to children for the joy and nourishment of stories, not as a vehicle for teaching literacy. The literacy benefits are in addition to this joy of engagement with storybooks.

As with children's emersion in, and engagement with, environmental print, reading storybooks to children will draw them into an awareness of print: what it is, how it works and what it is used for. Additionally, Clay (1991) observes that books teach about story schema, plot structure, anticipation of events, recall of previous story reading and the ways in which language is used to create the effects of suppose, climax and humour. Children who have been read to will also become aware of the language of books: that the language of books is different from spoken language.

Print awareness in the digital environment

To be fully literate, children need to be digitally literate. In settings and schools we have always offered opportunities for children to engage with traditional print-based texts and tools, and many children have similar opportunities at home. However, as digital technology is now part of life, children also need opportunities to develop this aspect of their literacy. At home and in their community it is highly likely that children will have opportunities to become aware of print in the digital environment through the use of phones, computers, tablets, game consoles and other electronic devices.

This more inclusive definition of literacy also needs to be a feature of children's experience in settings and at school to enable them to develop the necessary breadth of print awareness. This issue was explored by Beschorner and Hutchison (2013) in their study 'iPads as a Literacy Teaching Tool in Early Education'. In the light of the increasing influence of digital technologies in literacy, they wanted to consider how iPads, or similar tablets, can be used in a developmentally appropriate manner with young children. Their study, which investigated the use of iPads in two pre-school classrooms with four- and five-year-old children, concluded that providing iPads, in addition to traditional print, enabled the children to extend their print awareness interacting with, organising and analysing meanings of the print in this situational context. They became familiar with the icon for apps and were able to navigate their way around the screen, even supporting others to find and access apps on their own screen. In addition, the iPads supported children's emergent writing. Beschorner and Hutchinson found that the children

> created varying forms of writing in the digital environment of the iPad. For example, children were able to write using letters or symbols and/or write drawings using several apps. The Doodle Buddy and Drawing Pad apps were both frequently used by students to write messages using letters and/or drawings formed on the screen using their finger, typed text using the keyboard, digital stickers or stamps, and photographs taken with the iPad.

> (Beschorner and Hutchinson, 2013, p6)

The iPads were used to send images to parents via email, enhancing children's understanding of the functions of print. And the use of the iPads encouraged children's talk and social interaction. Overall, Beschorner and Hutchinson (2013) concluded that the use of iPads was successful in supporting children's print awareness in the digital environment.

> *Children use environmental print to navigate within and between apps, and can use the iPad to read, write, and talk about print. In addition, using the iPad frequently becomes a social activity for young children as they often talk and work together while using the tool. It is possible that the mobility of the iPad contributes to the socialization that takes place, because children can see the screens of other children easily and can manipulate the touchscreen in groups.*

(Beschorner and Hutchinson, 2013, p9)

Flewitt *et al.* (2015, p289) concluded similarly that well-planned, iPad-based literacy activities *offered rich opportunities for communication, collaborative interaction, independent learning, and for children to achieve high levels of accomplishment.* In addition, they enabled children to construct positive images of themselves in relation to literacy and, in some cases, led teachers to favourably re-evaluate children's literacy competence.

All these early print and conceptual understandings are important as the context for the emergence of early literacy in children's play, and then later when learning phonics. As Clay (1991) asserts, it is a widely held view that learning to read and write at school will be easier for children with rich early literacy experience than for a child with limited literacy experience.

What young children come to understand about print

A number of studies describe the understandings that young children develop from their engagement with print. The studies looked at the ways in which children begin to understand print, including their emerging understanding of the relationship between text and pictures, and their spatial awareness of print. Interestingly, the studies cited by Clay (1991) revealed consistency between children's developing understandings across different countries and cultures.

Children's early understanding of the relationship between text and pictures
Both Clay's (1975) study conducted in New Zealand and Ferrerio and Teberosky's (1982) study conducted in Argentina reached the same conclusion: children between the ages of four and six years old had developed a range of concepts about the relationship between text and pictures. By this age, the children could make a number of distinctions:

- drawing from writing;
- pictures from print;
- letters from numbers;

- letters from punctuation;

- letters from words.

Clay's (1991) and Mackenzie's (1985) work concluded that there are a series of steps and stages in children's development of these conceptual understandings.

The relationship between a picture and a word
- First the text and picture are not differentiated.

- Then the children expect the text to be a label for the picture.

- The text is expected to provide cues with which to confirm predictions based on the pictures.

The relationship between a picture and a sentence
- Initially, there was little appreciation that print was a transcript of oral language.

- Children constructed an oral text with inferred meaning from the pictures. The text imitated the style of reading, using intonation patterns and gestures. Clearly, to be able to do this the children must have observed readers reading aloud and been read to. At this stage when the same text was placed underneath different pictures, the same process occurred: the children generated an oral text based on the pictures.

- At the third stage, the children gave some thought to the graphic properties of the text. They expected the text to name things that were pictured, but only things in the pictures. To them, print represented sentences that they could associate with the pictures.

- Next, children made connections between a word that named something and selected graphic representations in the text. This stage depended on recognition of breaks between words in the enunciation of the sentence.

- Finally, print represented sentences associated with the picture and some correspondence was recognised between the segmentation of the spoken utterance and graphics in the text.

What is evident from these studies is that there is a journey towards an understanding of how print represents language and is recorded graphically in writing. Through engagement with print in the environment and in storybooks children need to progress towards this understanding, as becoming literate, including learning phonics, is underpinned by an understanding of this relationship between language and print. This is emphasised by Ferrerio and Tebrosky (1982 in Clay 1991, p33) who drew two important conclusions from their study of this relationship.

1. The conception of print as a label for the picture is an important moment in the child's understanding of written language because the child has begun to work out what kind of representational system written language is.

2. Attention to the formal properties of print and correspondence with sound segments is the final step in the progression, not the entry point to understanding what written language is.

Spatial orientation to reading

Children need to learn the conventions of written language: left to right and top to bottom orientations. Interestingly, Clay (1991) observed that young children who hadn't adopted conventional orientations to print were observed to have developed their own ideas for proceeding through text – for example, moving left to right, then right to left. These children had also established continuity in their approach, avoiding leaps and jumps and sweeps across the text. Studies (Clay, 1991) showed that the process became more complex when children got beyond the simple picture books with two or three lines of text, with children pondering which page to read first, or how to proceed through the book. Clearly, these conventions are arbitrary, defined within the particular writing system that children are exposed to within their families and communities, and children need to learn them. For some bilingual children, these conventions will be different in their different languages – for example, spatial orientation in Arabic and Hebrew is right to left, and in Japanese script it is in columns that are read from top to bottom down the columns, and from right to left.

The development of these orientations to print are contingent on mediated experiences with print. Simple, straightforward interactions as we engage with print alongside children will draw their attention to the spatial orientation of print – interactions such as pointing out the text and the pictures, tracking the print as we read, and using commentary to explain where we start reading and how we proceed through the text.

Since Clay's studies, the digital environment has developed, with significant changes in the types of print that children are exposed to: their roots of literacy now go beyond traditional print-based literacy. Print conventions in the digital environment don't always follow conventional patterns – for example, we read text in a non-linear way as we scroll up and down pages. However, there is evidence to suggest that children are readily able to absorb these different ways of interfacing with print (Beschorner and Hutchison, 2013), expanding their notions of print to include digital environment print. What is important is that children get a balance of experience with print, so that they have opportunities to engage with traditional and digital print in their early years in anticipation of later literacy learning.

It is, therefore, clear that children's early engagement with print in their environment, through books and in the digital environment, builds essential early concepts about print: what it is and how we use it. This print awareness enables children to come to later literacy learning, including phonics, with a clear context for the role of literacy in our lives and a range of concepts to support their learning. It is these early experiences with print that nourish the roots of literacy (Goodman, 1986).

Children learning about print

Early print awareness leads into emergent literacy (Neumann *et al.*, 2011). Emergent literacy is a way of conceptualising early reading and writing behaviours that precede and develop into conventional literacy. Hall (1997) suggests that there are four reasons for referring to this process as emergent.

- The term indicates that the development of a child as a literacy user comes from within. It is children, supported by adults, who make sense of the print which surrounds them.

- Emergence implies a gradual process that takes place over time.

- Emergence focuses on the abilities that children have to make sense of the world, perceiving them as active in their learning rather than passive recipients of knowledge.

- Literacy only emerges if the conditions are right, so there has to be meaningful engagement with print and adults who support this for it to emerge. This also implies that early attempts at reading and writing must be respected and accepted as they are indicative of an emerging capability and need to be encouraged.

We can observe young children's emerging awareness of functions and forms of literacy in reading and writing behaviours that appear in their play. These reading and writing behaviours are evidence of children's attempts to make sense and meaning of the literacy practices that they have observed and been involved in. Children's activity and play thus acts as a vehicle for exploring functions and forms of print and, in turn, shows us just how much young children know about reading and writing. Literacy learning, therefore, is seen as taking place in the home, within communities and in pre-school settings as well as in school.

Print awareness and children who are bilingual

Bialystok (2001) argues that if we accept the premise that literacy emerges through print awareness and emergent literacy practices, there are no special contingencies for children who speak more than one language. Bilingual children will develop an understanding of the functions and forms of print and enter into literacy in the same way as all other children: through engagement with print in their environment, the digital environment and through storybook reading. The difference for young bilingual children is the exposure to two or more writing systems about which they need to develop understandings about print.

Clearly, children need to be able to read texts in the context of schooling so, in addition to their home language(s), they need the literacy skills in the majority language, and the cognitive skills that lead into reading in that language (Bialystok, 2001). Some complexities arise where there are divergences between the printed forms of the home language(s) that a child is learning and the language of schooling. As Bialystok comments:

> *Each language bears a slightly different relation to its printed form, each writing system represents spoken language in a somewhat different manner, each social group places a different premium on literacy and provides different levels of access to it, and each education system resolves the pedagogical issues independently.*

> (Bialystok, 2001, p154)

Therefore, many bilingual children will be developing their print awareness within differing writing systems. These may have similarities with English – for example, they may be based on the alphabetic principle – or there may be significant differences – for example, languages such as Chinese which have a logographic writing system.

However, there is evidence to suggest that exposure to different print and writing systems has significant advantages in establishing the necessary concepts about print that lead into literacy. This, Bialystok (2001) suggests, comes from the cognitive demands of exposure to different writing systems.

In summary, therefore, children who are bilingual need the same range of experiences with print, mediated by adults, in both (or all of) their languages, to ensure that they develop the necessary conceptual understandings about the forms and functions of print.

DEVELOP YOUR UNDERSTANDING

Bialystok (2001) discusses some of the ways in which the processes within writing systems differ. Develop your understanding about the different types of writing systems that exist: alphabetic, syllabic and logographic.

- Why is it important that you have this knowledge?

- What are the implications for bilingual children as they become aware of print?

- How might this help you to understand children's misconceptions and misunderstandings?

- In what ways will this knowledge influence your interactions with young children as they become increasingly aware of print?

- How can you support bilingual children and their families in this awareness?

Emergent literacy in the home

Research evidence shows that children who come to formal literacy learning with a high chance of success have particular early experiences in the home. Shea (2011) cites evidence that shows that children need interactive models of literacy: playful engagement in literate activities, support in the literacy tasks they choose, and the time and space to experiment in their own way. The EPPE study (2003) concluded that what parents do in the home is more important than who they are, and this evidence shows that this is particularly important for early literacy development.

Most children will grow up with literacy practices in their homes as part of their everyday lives, for example:

- recognising and making sense of print in the environment: signs, logos, captions, labels, brands;

- sharing books with adults;

- observing adults and older siblings reading for information and pleasure: books, magazines and newspapers, and online;

- games and apps on computers, tablets or hand-held devices;

- being apprentice to adult and older family members' uses of literacy in everyday life: reading, writing and sending emails and text messages; completing home-work; using social media; writing lists and reading letters; using the Internet to search for and read information;

- using early scribble and marks that have meaning – for example, signing a birthday card;

- using knowledge about literacy in play – for example, writing labels and captions, texting, talking on the phone, working on a computer.

This early engagement with print in their everyday lives is evident in what we can observe in children's emerging literacy. For example, children who have been read to can be observed modelling these behaviours, including book handling, and the pattern and intonation of storybook reading. In their role play they will 'pretend' to read the print, and in the environment they will recognise and 'read' familiar script such as super-market and brand names. It has also been observed that children's drawing and writing often reflect the scripts that they are exposed to and the patterns of organisation that are used in the print – for example, Harste *et al.* (1982) asked four-year-old children from a wide variety of international backgrounds to write down everything that they could write. None of the children could write recognisable words, yet their samples reflected an emerging understanding of the orthography of their language: the English-speaking child wrote in cursive-like scribbles, the Israeli child in marks that reflected the Hebrew alphabet and the Arab child commented that the researchers would not be able to read her script as her language has more dots than English. In terms of patterns of organisa-tion, Clay (1975) notes that children often use the recurring principle in their emergent writing in ways that reflect specific visual qualities of writing systems – for example, repeating pictures and letter-like shapes, or making longer messages by using clusters of shapes and letters or repeated words. Children's names are particularly significant to them in their early print awareness (*see* Scharer and Zutell, 2013, p454) often acting as an anchor for a child's understanding that *a specific written form consistently represents a particular meaning* (Scharer and Zutell, 2013, p454).

However, just being exposed to literacy practices has limited benefits for literacy development, because parents need to mediate these experiences to engage children in literacy practices (Neumann *et al.*, 2009). Children's attention needs to be drawn to aspects of literacy, and they need to be offered opportunities to engage with environ-mental print and emergent reading and writing.

- *Environmental print.* Children need to be encouraged to notice environmental print. It needs to be pointed out and read to them. Children need to be encour-aged to 'have a go' at understanding or reading the logos or print. Children's attempts at reading and understanding print in their environment need to be praised and encouraged.

- *Emergent reading.* Children need to have books read to them. They need to be introduced to book structure through their parents' use of the terminology and to story language and structure through hearing stories. Children need to talk about books and stories; they need time to go back through and over stories to label, discuss, comment and recall the story. They need to be encouraged to get involved in storytelling, initially through looking at the pictures, and then by recalling and retelling the story. The same approach is needed for non-fiction texts, digital books and stories, and rhymes and poems. These should be read to children and talked about, and the children should be encouraged to retell them.

- *Emergent writing.* Children need to be encouraged to notice when people are writing, have it explained why we write, and watch the writing process. They need to have opportunities provided for them to draw, paint, model, stick and use this in their play to represent their ideas. Ideally, they need opportunities to use technology in order to explore print in the digital environment. As children become interested in letters and they begin to appear in what they produce, they need support in understanding letter sounds and how letters are formed: they need to hear words sounded out and watch letters being formed correctly as they are written. This teaching needs to be matched to the children's interests and abilities, and be done in an authentic way in the context of their play and activities.

Neumann *et al.* (2009) present a case study of interaction in the home that facilitates emergent literacy skills.

WHAT DOES RESEARCH TELL US?

The scaffolding of emergent literacy skills in the home environment: a case study (Neumann et al., 2009)

Neumann *et al.*'s (2009) study focused on describing strategies used by one parent during interactions that made use of environmental print and joint writing activities. They describe the child and family in this way:

> Harry was from a middle income family. Both parents (first and third authors) had tertiary education and professional occupations. Harry's cognitive and physical development was normal. Harry did not experience any letter drills, phonetic instruction, or formal reading teaching prior to school entry.

> (Neumann et al., 2009, p314)

Parental approaches

From an early age, Harry was provided with many repetitive opportunities to engage with the same print on food packages, branding on objects and clothes, and written materials. From when he was two, Harry's mother began to mediate his engagement with print, scaffolding his ability to distinguish print from pictures and photos on environmental print. This was accompanied by vocalising the words, running her finger under the print to demonstrate where it was, naming the letters and demonstrating how they are formed in large arm movements, encouraging Harry to join in.

(Continued)

From the age of 2½ years, Harry began to spontaneously point out environmental print. He was able to point to pictures and name them and identify the print, using his term 'up-downs'.

Once Harry was able to differentiate environmental print from pictures and understood that print carried meaning, his mother increasingly focused on individual letters within the print. She used a multisensory approach, encouraging Harry to look at the print, listen to his mother say the word and letter, and form the letter in the air with large arm movement. In addition, Harry's mother identified other words that started with the same letter.

Play activities supported this interaction: shaping letters in playdough or cookie dough, and play with plastic and magnetic letters. The parents and family also encouraged and commented on letter shapes that occurred elsewhere – for example, an E made out of fish fingers, an O from rope and a V from sticks. Letters were also identified when reading storybooks.

Harry was also provided with opportunities to scribble and draw from as soon as he could grasp a crayon – for example, at age two he was encouraged to draw large up and down, around and across marks on a chalkboard, and by three he was making marks on paper. As Harry made marks on paper and chalkboard, his mother described what he was doing with directional words – up down, across and around. Neumann *et al.* make a direct link to Harry's early experiences with environmental print.

> *This pre-writing gross motor activity helped Harry link these physical experiences with his previous encounters with environmental print where he had visually explored and physically traced vertically positioned letters using directional language (up, down, around, and across).*
>
> (Neumann *et al.*, 2009, p316)

Throughout these early experiences with environmental print and joint writing activities, Harry was highly motivated. He responded enthusiastically during interactions. Additionally, there was no sense of frustration as Harry seemed aware that his mother would scaffold his learning, using the familiar movements and terms up–down–across–around.

By the age of six, Harry had made substantial progress.

> *Harry evidenced phonetic spelling by saying the sound of letters in words and writing them down. He could independently write in sentence form using correct upper and lower case letters. Harry no longer needed to sign shapes in the air or say their directions aloud. Harry had internalized the ability to write letters and words. However, Harry could occasionally be heard whispering the directions of*

(Continued)

some letters when he wrote independently at home. Winsler and Naglieri (2003) described this progression from external speech via whispering and silent lip movements to fully internal or private speech as a characteristic developmental pattern observable as children complete challenging tasks.

The researchers concluded that guided exposure to environmental print proved to be a really useful tool to help Harry develop the visual skills needed to orientate towards print and acquire early alphabetic knowledge. They found that environmental print provided abundant stimulus to motivate Harry to become aware of print and letters.

The authors acknowledge that this interaction is predicated upon strong parent–child relationships and secure attachment – frequency of shared reading and activities such as pointing, labelling and commenting are associated with positive patterns of attachment. It also requires a certain degree of sensitivity, responsiveness and guidance by parents who need to be alert to the child's attention to environmental print and capitalise on these opportunities as they arise. However, the authors also note that the advantage of this approach is that it is embedded within everyday activities such as shopping, eating and travelling, so is not burdensome in terms of time. Additionally, they comment that this approach may be suitable for parents with low levels of literacy as most adults can identify common environmental print and individual letters.

DEVELOP YOUR UNDERSTANDING

A number of researchers have highlighted the fact that discussion around, and assessment of, literacy at home is dominated by school-based literacy. School-based literacy, they argue, is so dominant in how we understand literacy that it is regarded as the 'real one' and all other literacies (community literacy, literacies of popular culture, intergenerational literacy and family literacy (Knobel and Lankshear, 2003)) are regarded as less important or less valid. This, it is argued, disadvantages children who arrive in school with different literacy experiences.

Purcell Gates (1995, p9) observes a *chilling picture* of the way in which this dominance serves to block access to literacy for some children because a particular type of home-based literacy is so significant for the acquisition of school-based literacy. Likewise, Brookner (2003) concluded that children have varying degrees of success in importing their home literacy into the classroom. She argues that, from the two cases she studied, both of which had considerable literacy experiences at home, only one child's assets were in the appropriate currency to be invested in the official education system.

Yaden *et al.*'s conclusions (2000) focused on the socially embedded nature of children's writing. They comment that the studies they reviewed highlighted the cultural and interactive basis of how children use and define literacy, and note that this raises complex issues

(Continued)

118

concerning *societal values and definitions of literacy, clashes of culture between home and school and differential valuing of the cultural capital that children bring to school* (Yaden *et al.*, 2000, p437).

- Why do you think that school literacy is so dominant?

- Why do some children arrive in school with different literacy experiences?

- Why does this mean that some children can access school learning easily while others find it more difficult?

- What does this mean for provision in pre-school settings? Does it mean that pre-schools should exist to prepare children for school, or are they there for a different purpose? What are the benefits and difficulties with each of these approaches?

Emergent literacy in the setting

Pre-school settings need to provide literacy-rich experiences. Developmentally appropriate literacy provision in pre-school settings should be similar to authentic literacy interactions in children's homes (Shea, 2011). However, in contrast to homes and communities there are fewer naturally occurring opportunities for authentic literacy experiences in settings and schools. Therefore, practitioners need to provide a literate environment in which children can engage in contextualised literacy practices and adopt pedagogical approaches that model, encourage and teach literacy.

A positive literacy-learning environment needs to be print-rich. There needs to be extensive use of labelling, captions and instructions. Books need to be readily available and regularly read to the children. Opportunities for literacy in routines needs to be used to engage children in literacy practices – for example, self-registration, sign-up sheets for computer use, labelled boxes for tidying up. Neuman and Roskos's (1992) seminal paper demonstrates the impact of providing opportunities for literacy in children's play.

WHAT DOES RESEARCH TELL US?

Literacy objects as cultural tools: effects on children's literacy behaviours in play (Neumann and Roskos, 1992)

Neuman and Roskos (1992) were interested in how organisation of the learning environment might influence children's opportunities to engage in literacy learning. They argue that Gump's (1989) assertion that the physical environment can 'coerce' behaviour has important implications for literacy learning in early childhood – that we may be able to

(Continued)

extend the range of literacy opportunities for young children and thereby encourage developmentally appropriate literacy activities. Given this potential of the learning environment, Neuman and Roskos (1992) were interested in whether or not changes in the structural features of the play environment would have consequences for children's emerging conceptions of literacy.

The study compared pre-school-aged children's behaviours in two settings: an intervention setting that was reorganised and enriched with literacy objects, and a non-intervention setting which remained as it was. Methods included assessment of children's awareness of print before and after intervention, video recording of children's play and researcher observation. It was designed to answer the following questions.

- Do play settings enriched with literacy objects influence the frequency of literacy demonstrations in the spontaneous play of pre-schoolers?

- Does the inclusion of literacy objects in play environments influence the duration and complexity of literacy-related free play?

- How are literacy objects used in children's spontaneous play?

They found that the infusion of literacy objects, alongside physical changes in the organisation of the setting, significantly influenced the nature of children's literacy behaviours. The children in the intervention group spent more time in handling, reading and writing activities in play than the non-intervention group. This involvement with literacy became more sustained and interconnected as literacy was increasingly integrated into their play themes over the seven-month period of the study. In addition, children in the intervention group relied more often on the language of literacy over gesture, and incorporated literacy into their play in more diverse and functional ways.

Neuman and Roskos (1992) conclude that the *coercive power* that the learning environment exerts over children is important: that deliberate enrichment of the play environment with familiar literacy objects in equally familiar contexts of literacy use enhanced children's literacy activity in play. Significantly, the frequency, duration and complexity of the children's playful literacy activity increased, suggesting that the literacy objects encouraged self-generated literacy activity.

Pedagogy of emergent literacy

In addition to the provision of a print-rich environment, practitioners need to plan activities and experiences that enable children to engage in emergent reading and engage in representation through drawing, modelling, mark making and role-play. This requires that careful thought is given to how literacy can be incorporated into activities in an authentic, contextualised way. This is important. Children need to learn about why we read and write as well as how we read and write. Play that mimics real uses of literacy communicates why we need to read and write. For example, in a role-play take-away pizza shop, children can engage with a range of environmental print in the shop and on the boxes and delivery vehicles, read the menus and write down orders and addresses using their emerging literacy skills.

Teachers and practitioners need to get involved in the activities alongside children and adopt pedagogical practices that actively engage children in using their nascent literacy knowledge and skills.

- *Encourage reading and writing*

  Playing alongside children and getting involved in modelling where when and how reading and writing are used will show children how literacy is part of the activity and encourage them to incorporate this in their play.

- *Model reading and writing*

  Pointing out print, words and letters, tracking the lines of print, and sounding out words when reading, and allowing children to see us writing will model the processes of reading and writing.

- *Verbalise phonic sounds*

  Where appropriate, and in context, we should verbalise letter sounds (phonemes) and blend and segment words. This models the process of synthetic phonics. Using teachable moments (moments where we notice that there is the opportunity to teach a concept or skill in context as the child is ready and/or needs to know) is an appropriate pedagogical strategy for modelling reading and writing, and teaching children about letter sounds, segmenting and blending, and letter formation.

Stages of emergent reading and writing

Broad patterns of development can be seen in children's emerging literacy skills. These are useful for tracking children's developing knowledge and skill to ensure that our provision and interaction is closely mapped to the abilities and needs of the children. However, as always with developmental trajectories, we need to be cautious in how we use and apply them. The most persistent criticism of developmentalism is that it is decontextualized – that is, it doesn't allow for the different contexts in which children grow and learn. Developmentalism seeks to identify very broad, general patterns of development and apply these to all children regardless of their life experiences. Therefore, it is argued, that the approach is too unsubtle to understanding every child's growth and development (Dahlberg *et al.*, 1999; Baker, 1999). Additionally, there is the risk that normative descriptions of children's development become prescriptions for what 'should' happen and judgements are made about children based on these assumptions. Burman (2008) and Baker (1999) identify the potential impact of this, arguing that when developmental parameters are articulated and set down, the visibility of expectations means that children can be segregated into those who meet expectations and those who don't. Normative descriptions are then used to classify and stratify individuals, groups and societies, so, by intention or default, we create inclusion and exclusion.

Emergent reading

Sulzby and Rockafellow (2001) provide a framework that traces the development of emergent reading from the earliest engagement with storybooks through to independent reading. She observes that children's reading of books emerges initially through simple labelling and commenting based on the pictures, through a series of stages in which a child learns and refines story-telling language, to reading that uses emerging understanding of phonics and other word-recognition skills to support story telling from a book.

Stages of emergent reading
Picture-governed attempts
Labels or responds to the pictures on each page with little or no understanding of the whole story.
Telling the story based on the picture in front of them. The story told is based on the actual story but the language of storytelling and the book is not used
Children will tell the story using both the pictures and the language of the story that they have learned from hearing the story over and over again. Their emergent reading begins to sound like conventional reading. This indicates that the child is becoming aware of, and making a transition between oral language and written language.
Print-governed attempts
Children will attempt to read the book using the print. This indicates that they have learned that it is the print that carries the story when adults read rather than the pictures. Some children will have remembered the story exactly and appear to read the print, while others will insist on reading the print but still struggle to decode it.
Children will bring together what they know about print and what they remember of the text and pictures to read the text conventionally.

Table 6.1   Stages of emergent reading: picture- and print-governed attempts

Sulzby's (1985) work focused on emergent reading using storybooks. The same patterns can be observed in children's engagement with non-fiction texts, digital print and with rhymes and poems. Children will label and list before beginning to use some of the language of the text and eventually, from repeated exposure to the text, use what they know about print and what they remember of the text to read it conventionally.

Emergent writing

As with emergent reading, the pattern of progress in emergent writing can be observed. Emergent writing is predominantly concerned with the process and content of writing rather than handwriting. Through engagement with print in their environment children become aware of letters and sounds and begin to shape their understanding of writing. Scharer and Zutell (2013) note that there are many levels of understanding that young children need to develop, over time, to enable them to move into writing conventionally. These include:

- the relationship between oral language and writing;
- how pronunciation and meaning of oral linguistic units are mapped to particular written forms;
- that written symbols are different from objects or pictures;
- the complex characteristics of writing system(s) such as directionality and the concept of a word;
- the features of the script(s) that accompany the language(s) they speak;
- specific rules and patterns of the orthography/orthographies;
- that writing systems have a consistency.

Therefore, development is unlikely to just happen on its own; it requires adults to model, encourage and teach when appropriate and where necessary, and the opportunity for children to rehearse emerging knowledge and skill. Therefore, prior to children engaging in representation that approximates to conventional writing, they will need to have had sustained exposure to environmental print and engaged in play-based activities to enable them to learn, develop, and consolidate their ability to symbolise in concrete contexts (*see* Chapter 7).

Stages of emergent writing	
Scribbling	Emergent writing begins with first explorations in mark making often for purposes other than representation. These are random scribbles or marks on a page, on steamy windows, in sand or mud with sticks. Very young children will use the words, drawing and writing interchangeably to describe the marks. Children age 3–4 have usually begun to differentiate between the two.
Mock handwriting or wavy scribble	Children produce lines of wavy scribbles in imitation of adult writing. The writing often appears on a page with drawing. This pretend writing also often appears in children's role-play within an appropriate context, such as writing an appointment in a book. Children tend to do the imitation writing in large amounts, sometimes covering a page.
Mock letters	Children attempt to form alphabetic letters. These tend to be letter-like shapes that resemble conventional letters. They appear in their writing and their drawing. Research has shown that these scribbles and letter-like shapes take on the characteristics of the print in a child's culture – scribbles in Hebrew and Arabic, for example, look very different from scribbles in English (Harste *et al.*, 1984).
Conventional letters	Children's mock letters gradually become more conventional and letters appear in what they produce. These early experiments with real letters are usually the letters in their names or close family members' names. Children often create strings of letters across a page and 'read' them as a sentence or series of sentences. The letters appear on drawings as the child's signature or as a label for the drawing. Environmental print has a particular importance at this stage as children increasingly begin to notice the detail of letters and print.

(Continued)

Table 6.2   (Continued)

Stages of emergent writing	
Invented spelling	Once children are comfortable with writing conventional individual letters, they begin to cluster them together to make word forms. They often do not look like or sound like 'real' words. Children will often ask, 'What did I write?'
Approximated (phonetic) spelling	Children attempt to spell words based on their growing awareness of letter sounds (phonemes) and their sight vocabulary of words that they have seen repeatedly. These beginning words are often written in a random combination of upper and lower case letters, depending on the child's knowledge and skill. Children move from spelling words using the beginning letter, to writing both beginning and final letters, to writing words with the appropriate beginning, middle and final letters.
Conventional spelling	Children's approximated spellings gradually become more and more conventional. The child's own name is usually written first.

Table 6.2   More stages of emergent reading

(Adapted from Project ELIPSS)

WHAT DOES RESEARCH TELL US?

Gnys at wrk (Bissex, 1980)

Glenda Bissex undertook a study (1980) that documented her son's emergent writing. She became fascinated by his invented spelling and what this indicated about his understanding of writing.

Paul, her son, lived in a house full of print and frequently saw his parents reading. He had had stories read aloud to him since he was a baby and had a collection of his own books. Paul had wooden and magnetic letters and rubber letter stamps among his playthings. His family had not taught him letters and sounds formally, but letters were frequently pointed out and referred to. Paul had watched Sesame Street since he was three years old which, again, informally introduced him to letters and letter sounds. Paul was an only child and lived in the country, which meant that he had significant periods of solitude to play and concentrate without interruption. Paul's first attempt at writing was a welcome home banner for his mum. It consisted of a random string of letters: z z H i D C A.

Paul was familiar with both upper and lower case letters but he chose, and preferred, to use capital letters. Bissex argues that this may be because they have visual primacy with children; capitals are more distinctive; they retain their identity even when reversed; they are used for important communication in conventional writing.

Paul's earliest attempts at writing were not attempts to spell or to print letters but to communicate: the welcome home banner, a note to a friend and a page of green letters to make his mum 'feel better'. This continued as his writing developed. The writing had a purpose, often in play, but always as an act of communication.

(Continued)

Paul's emergent writing ability can be observed in examples of his writing that reflect his growing awareness of print: the purposes for writing and the forms of writing. Over a period of seven months, Paul made the following progress:

RUDF - Are you deaf?

PAULSTLEFNMBR – Paul's telephone number

DOTGATNERA KOR – Don't get near a car.

I WILL TECH U TO RIT AD THES EZ HAOW – I will teach you to write and this is how

DO NAT DSTRB GNYS AT WORK – Do not disturb genius at work

THA. BEG. EST. HOS. EN. THA. WRALD – The biggest house in the world

PAUL. IS GOWING. TO. RUN. A. RAWN. AND. JUMP. AND EXRSICS – Paul is going to run and run and jump and exercise

What is important about Bissex's research is her conclusion that learning to write is a non-linear process – it does not follow a regular, predictable, step-by-step process. It was a process that engaged with the child's interests and abilities. What was evident throughout her observations was the importance of exposure to literacy practices, embedded within everyday life, and the on-going interaction with the adults who matched their interaction to his interests and guided him towards conventional literacy.

Getting parents involved

Children's roots of literacy lie in their earliest experiences with print in which they come to know the functions and forms of reading and writing. Some of this will take place in settings, but much will also take place at home and in a child's community. Parents therefore need to know how they can support their child's early print awareness and encourage their emergent reading and writing.

Developing print awareness and encouraging children's emergent literacy can be integrated into everyday life (Neumann *et al.*, 2009) – for example, while we shop, eat, text, travel, cook, walk and engage with social media. What is important is that parents are aware of the ways in which they can support their child's early literacy. This may include the following.

Environmental print. Encourage parents to point out, read and discuss print on, for example, clothing, packaging, toys, supermarket logos and menus. Encourage children to recognise familiar words and logos. One nursery found that a bingo-type game supported these discussions: the children were given cards showing logos and/or environmental print and were encouraged to look for them at home and on their journey to and from school. Where they had seen them, what they understood by them, and the images and print used were then a focus for discussion in the nursery.

Model reading and writing. Encourage parents to point out when they are reading or writing and let children observe them doing it. Encourage parents to track the print as they read, and say the letter sounds as they read and write. Emphasise that this can be done incidentally, as they read labels, text, signs and instructions.

Story reading. The importance of books and reading to children cannot be underestimated. As well as reading through the story and making the time together enjoyable, parents can be encouraged to point out the pictures and the print, track the print as they read and say some letter sounds.

Encouraging children's early efforts at engaging with print. It is important that parents praise and support children's early efforts at engaging with print. Children's early efforts at understanding print, mark making and letter naming are unlikely to be conventionally correct, but are part of the process of moving towards conventional literacy that needs to be encouraged. Continuing to model the functions and forms of print, with a drip feed, day-by-day approach, will develop children's print awareness and lead into later school-based literacy learning.

Conclusion

This chapter has looked at what we mean by print awareness and what children learn about the functions and forms of print from their engagement with print, including digital print. It has outlined how children can learn about the digital environment in meaningful ways, both at home and in settings. It has considered print awareness for children who are growing up bilingual. Ways in which parents can be encouraged to support children's print awareness in their everyday interactions have also been discussed.

References

Ashton, J (2010) Book review: Fellowes, J and Oakley, G *Language, Literacy and Early Childhood Education*. Victoria: Oxford University Press. *Journal of Early Childhood Literacy*, 13(1): 131–7. Available online at: **http://434759422212416091.weebly.com/ uploads/2/9/3/7/29371713/journal_of_early_childhood_literacy-2013-ashton-131-7.pdf** (accessed 11 September 2016).

Baker, B (1999) The dangerous and the good? Developmentalism, progress and public schooling. *American Education Research Journal*, 36(4): 797–834.

Beschorner, B and Hutchison, A (2013) iPads as a literacy teaching tool in early childhood. *International Journal of Education in Mathematics, Science and Technology*, 1(1): 16–24. Available online at: **http://ijemst.com/issues/2_Beschorner_Hutchison_.pdf** (accessed 11 September 2016).

Bialystok, E (2001) *Bilingualism in Development: Language, Literacy and Cognition*. Cambridge: Cambridge University Press.

Bissex, G (1980) *Gnys at Wrk: A Child Learns to Write and Read*. London: Harvard University Press.

Brookner, L (2003) Five on the first of December: What we can learn from case studies of early childhood literacy. *Journal of Early Childhood Literacy*, 2(3): 291–313.

Burman, E (2008) *Deconstructing Developmental Psychology*. London: Routledge.

Clay, M (1975) in Scharer, P and Zutell, J (2013) The Development of Spelling, in Larson, J and Marsh, J (2013) *SAGE Handbook of Early Childhood Literacy*. London: SAGE.

Clay, M (1991) *Becoming Literate: The Construction of Inner Control*. London: Heinemann.

Dahlberg, G, Moss, P and Pence, A (1999) *Beyond Quality in Early Childhood and Care: Postmodern Perspectives*. London: Falmer Press.

ELIPSS project (no date) Available online at: **http://thesimplicityoflearning2013.blogspot.co.uk/2013_11_01_archive.html**

EPPE (2003) Sylva, K, Melhuish, E, Sammons, P, Siraj Blatchford, I, Taggart, B and Elliot, K (2003) Effective Provision of Pre-School (EPPE) Project: Findings from the Pre-School Period. **http://eppe.ioe.ac.uk/eppe/eppepdfs/eppe_brief2503.pdf** (accessed 11 September 2016).

Ferrerio, E and Teberosky, A (1982) in Clay, M (1991) *Becoming Literate: The Construction of Inner Control*. London: Heinemann.

Flewitt, R, Messer, D and Kucirkova, N (2015) New directions for early literacy in a digital age: The iPad. *Journal of Early Childhood Literacy*, 15(3): 289–310.

Goodall, M (1984) Can four year olds 'read' words in the environment? *Reading Teacher*, 37(6): 478–89.

Goodman, Y (1986) Children Coming to Know Literacy. In Teale, W and Sulzby E (1986) *Emergent Literacy Reading and Writing*. Norwood, NJ: Ablex Publishing Corporation.

Hall, N (1997) *The Emergence of Literacy*. Sevenoaks: Hodder & Stoughton.

Harste, J, Burke, CL and Woodward, VA (1982) in Scharer, P and Zutell, J (2013) The Development of Spelling. In Larson, J and Marsh, J (2013) *SAGE Handbook of Early Childhood Literacy*. London: SAGE.

Knobel, M and Lankshear, C (2003) *New Literacies*. Milton Keynes: Open University Press.

Mackenzie, T (1985) in Clay, M (1991) *Becoming Literate: The Construction of Inner Control*. London: Heinemann.

Neuman, S and Roskos, K (1992) Literacy objects as cultural tools: Effects on children's literacy behaviours in play. *Reading Research Quarterly*, 27(3): 202–25. Available online at: **www-personal.umich.edu/~sbneuman/pdf/LiteracyObjects.pdf** (accessed 11 September 2016).

Neumann, MM, Hood, M, Neumann, DL (2009) The scaffolding of emergent literacy skills in the home environment: A case study. *Early Childhood Education Journal*, 36(4): 313–19.

Neumann, MM, Hood, M, Ford, RM and Neumann, DL (2011) The role of environmental print in emergent literacy. *Journal of Early Childhood Literacy*, 12(3): 231–58.

Purcell Gates, V (1995) *Other People's Words: The Cycle of Low Literacy*. London: Harvard University Press.

Scharer, P and Zutell, J (2013) The development of spelling. In Larson, J and Marsh, J (2013) *SAGE Handbook of Early Childhood Literacy*. London: SAGE.

Shea, M (2011) *Parallel Learning of Reading and Writing in Early Childhood*. London: Routledge.

Sulzby, E (no date) Stages of children's writing. Available online at: **www.wiu.edu/itlc/ws/ws1/docs/Stages_of_%20ChildWrit.pdf** (accessed 11 September 2016).

Sulzby, E (1985) Children's emergent reading of storybooks: A developmental study. *Reading Research Quarterly*, 20(4): 458–81.

Sulzby, E and Rockafellow, B (2001) Sulzby classification scheme instructional profiles. Available online at: **www.binghamtonschools.org/Downloads/Sulzby'sEmergentStoryBookReading.pdf** (accessed 11 September 2016).

Sulzby, E and Teale, WH (1991) Emergent literacy. In Barr, R, Kamil, M, Mosenthal, P and Pearson, PD (1991) *Handbook of Reading Research, Volume 2*. Mahwah, NJ: Lawrence Erlbaum Associates.

Sylva, K, Melhuish, E, Sammons, P, Siraj Blatchford, I, Taggart, B and Elliot, K (2003) Effective Provision of Pre-School (EPPE) project: Findings from the pre-school period. Available online at: **www.ucl.ac.uk/ioe/research/featured-research/effective-pre-school-primary-secondary-education-project/publications** (accessed 11 September 2016).

Yaden, D, Rowe, D and MacGillivray, L (1999) Emergent literacy: A polyphony of perspectives. CIERA. Available online at: **www.ciera.org/library/reports/inquiry-1/1-005/1-005.html** (accessed 11 September 2016).

7 Symbolising and representation

Introduction

The ability to represent the world symbolically is fundamental to becoming literate.

This chapter examines what is meant by the ability to represent the world symbolically and how this leads into phonics teaching and learning. It considers this issue for children who are bilingual. Interaction, activities and experiences that support the ability to symbolise are outlined.

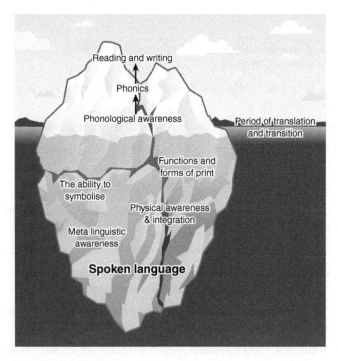

Figure 7.1   What comes before phonics

What do we mean by symbolising and representation?

Look at your hands. Touch them, feel them, and rub them together. These sensations are sensorimotor experiences. You are using your senses of touch and sight to experience the world: it is a real experience of your hands.

We can also recognise hands in various other forms. Look at the images below. These are all symbolic representations of the physical object of a hand: a line drawing, a photograph, a 3D sculpture and a symbol.

Clearly, none of these is an actual hand. They are symbols for a hand. They are all different but we can understand them as we can 'read' the symbol and understand what it is representing.

We can also represent the physical object of a hand in speech. In English, we use the phonemes *h/a/n/d* and blend them together to make the spoken word 'hand'. This blend of sounds stands as a symbol to represent our physical hand. Bilingual children will have two or more sound blends to represent their hand in speech.

We can also represent our hand with written symbols. Writing is the setting down of speech. It consists of a series of lines and curves on a page to represent speech. So, in English, we use this series of lines and curves – hand – to represent the word hand. In Hindi it is this series of lines and curves, हाथ. In Arabic it is يد. In Italian it is mano, and in Greek it is χέρι.

In anticipation of becoming literate, children need to learn how to recognise and represent things symbolically, and this is an important part of children's early development. Given appropriate opportunities, this ability will emerge and develop in their play and interaction with their families, community and in early years settings.

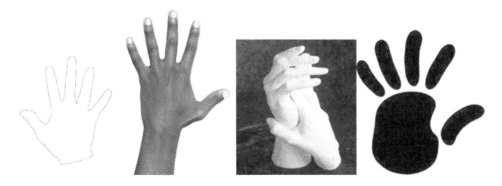

Figure 7.2 'Hands'

The ability to symbolise and phonics

The ability to use one thing to represent another is fundamental to literacy learning, including phonics. Writing is the symbolic representation of spoken language. Reading is understanding and decoding symbols that represent speech. So, put simply, phonics is about learning the symbolic basis of our system of reading and writing. It requires children to learn the correspondence between the symbols (letters) and the sounds (phonemes) that we use to symbolically represent spoken language. This ability develops through the early use of gesture, through learning to talk, through concrete experiences in play that require symbolic use of props and equipment, and through early mark making and drawing. The development of the ability to use symbols is an important aspect of what comes before phonics.

Vygotsky (in Rieber and Hall, 1997) makes a distinction between first-order and second-order symbolism. First-order symbols can be understood directly: the symbols directly signify the objects or actions, such as the images of the hand above. We can 'read' and understand these symbols for a hand as there is a direct relationship between what we see and the object that it represents.

Second-order symbolism is more complex. Second-order symbols are more indirect and opaque. In terms of literacy, they consist of *written signs for oral symbols of words* (Vygotsky in Rieber and Hall, 1997, p142). For example, we use the symbols h/a/n/d to represent the object of a hand, and when we see this symbol we recognise it as representing a hand.

However, if we were presented with the symbols χέρι it would have no meaning for us as English speakers and readers. We cannot understand these symbols. This is because these are second-order symbols, which means that these symbols bear no resemblance to the object of a hand. The symbols are indirect. We only recognise the relationship between the symbols and the object of a hand when it is written as 'hand' because we have learned the second-order symbolic system of English. People who are able to write and read in two or more languages will have two or more second-order symbolic systems to represent their languages. Children will learn the symbolic system(s) that are used in their family and community.

Phonics is a second-order symbolic system. When learning phonics, children must learn the indirect symbols that represent speech sounds. This shift from first-order to second-order symbolism is an important move in becoming literate. Young children need to have developed the necessary skills to enable them to transition from symbolic representation that has a direct and immediate meaning, to the more indirect symbolism required to learn phonics. Therefore, in the context of what comes before phonics, children need opportunities to develop the ability to symbolise, and then to begin to represent their understanding symbolically to enable them to access later phonics teaching with a good chance of success.

Interestingly, Vygotsky (in Rieber and Hall, 1997, p142) notes that once children have become fluently literate, there is an additional transition as second-order symbols in reading and writing transition to become first-order symbols. Once we are experienced and competent readers, the written word eventually comes to denote the things themselves. However, long before this happens children need to develop the ability to represent the world symbolically, and for this to become increasingly sophisticated to create a firm foundation for the later literacy learning.

WHAT DOES RESEARCH TELL US?

Bilingualism in development: language, literacy and cognition (Bialystok, 2001)

Bialystok (2001) notes a series of research studies that look at the detail of children's errors about the relationship between words and symbols. Her studies show that even as children move into becoming literate with good print awareness (*see* Chapter 6) and emerging phonological awareness (*see* Chapter 8), there are still aspects of the relationship between words and their symbolic representations that some children misunderstand.

Bialystok (2001, pp160–1) comments that *learning how to interpret symbol systems that are indirect, second order or opaque, is an important cognitive achievement and must certainly precede learning to read.*

- Ferrerio's work (1978, 1983, 1984, cited in Bialystok, 2001) indicated that children believed that print needed to embody the characteristics of the word – big objects should be represented by big letters and small objects by small letters. Groups of objects should be represented by groups of repeated letters or words. Bialystok (2001) interprets this as children looking for aspects of meaning in the visual properties of the printed forms, as you would in first-order symbolism.

- Bialystok looked at this misunderstanding using words where there was incongruity between the size of the word and the size of the object it names, for example, in the pair 'caterpillar-train', the longer word represents the shorter object. Her study confirmed aspects of Ferrerio's work – namely, it *showed that children with much background knowledge of print could not use the property of sound symbol correspondence to choose between long and short words* (Bialystok, 2001, pp162–3).

- Children also need to come to understand the invariance of notation: that words always represent the same thing regardless of how they are written. Bialystok (2001) gives the following example. A drawing of a dog can be changed to represent a different type of dog, or a part of the dog such as nose or wagging tail, or a bigger or smaller dog. Changing the picture changes (however slightly) the meaning. However, changing the word 'dog' by changing the size of the print or the font has no impact on the thing that it is representing.

Bialystok (2001) emphasises that children's insights about the way in which print represents text are part of the journey en route to literacy. There is no straight line from these preliminary skills to the attainment of autonomous literacy: it is simply one aspect that needs to be in place.

Other symbolic systems

In addition to language, reading and writing, we use a range of other symbolic systems. Vygotsky called these cultural tools. He noted that as humans we use various types of tools to extend and support our physical capabilities – for example, knives, forks and spoons – and in addition we use psychological tools to support and extend our mental abilities (Palmer, 2005). These are symbolic systems and as human beings we use a range of them. In addition to language and images (pictures) these include:

- signs;
- symbols;
- maps;
- plans;
- numbers;
- musical notation;
- charts;
- models.

Young children will need opportunities to engage with these at an appropriate level, as engagement in symbolic representation of all sorts builds their understanding and ability in this area.

Learning to represent the world symbolically

Initially, children come to know and begin to understand the world through being active: by exploring the world through their senses. These first-hand sensory experiences are known as the Sensorimotor Stage (Piaget and Inhelder, 1972). Observably, very young children pick things up, put them in their mouth, shake and bang them. All of this motor action builds children's understanding of the world. These emerging understandings are important as the early stages of conceptual development, which will later be represented symbolically. Representation occurs when sensorimotor assimilation becomes mental assimilation as symbolic representation is the ability to use mental symbols to represent objects and events (Stone and Stone, n.d.). Children's ability to represent the world symbolically continues and becomes increasingly sophisticated as they:

- use a wide range of gestures to communicate;
- acquire and develop spoken language;
- engage in play activities that require them to use one thing to represent another – for example, a piece of fabric for a cloak, a teddy for a baby, a skipping rope as horse reins, or play dough as food;
- begin mark making.

Early acquisition of language and early gestures begin the process of representing the world symbolically, as words and gestures are symbolic representations of objects and events. Early symbols include their own name and names of familiar people, and words that name and describe familiar activities, routines, toys and characters. Initially, this will be through imitation; then, through continued interaction, children will come to know that a particular word stands as a symbol for someone or something. Very young children also begin to recognise and respond with, and to, simple gestures, such a wave or a clap. Again, through contextualised use of these early gestures, children come to know that they act as symbols for other things, a wave to signal hello or goodbye, a blown kiss as a symbol of affection representing a real kiss, raised arms as a request to be picked up and carried, and clapping to express delight. Very quickly children learn to communicate using these symbols and we respond as we can 'read' the meaning of the symbol.

As children grow and develop and broaden their experiences, their ability to represent their understandings through the use of symbols emerges in different forms: in their play, as mark making and modelling, in music and in their movement. For example, in their play children may use loud sounds on instruments to represent something that is big, or exciting, or joyful, or fast. They may begin to make marks on paper, or in paint, or sand, and tell you what they represent. They may swish and swirl their body and tell you that they are river. This engagement in the representation of their thoughts, ideas and imaginings in symbolic ways is indicative of their developing ability to symbolise and, with experience and opportunity, this will become increasingly focused and sophisticated. As Vygotsky notes: *At that critical moment when a stick – i.e. an object – becomes a pivot for severing the meaning of horse from a real horse, one of the basic psychological structures determining the child's relationship to reality is radically altered* (1967, p12). Vygotsky's work has been highly influential in our understanding of symbolic play. He argued that one of the important accomplishments of their early years is children's growing ability to use a variety of signs and symbol systems – from gestures and words to drawing and written marks – that prepares them for the increasingly complex symbol systems they will learn in school (Bodrova and Leong, 2015). This, he argues is accomplished through symbolic (pretend, or imaginary) play, as this acts as a transitional stage from a child's thinking constrained by the properties of a current situation to thinking totally free from these constraints (Bodrova and Leong, 2015). Therefore, the use of symbolic representation in children's play activities is highly significant as it opens up possibilities for them to seek, make, express and represent meaning in their world.

Kress (1997) observes this, noting that children have huge scope to create meaning because, unlike adults who tend to use language to represent their ideas, children use a range of different modes. Very young children's early representations will be first-order representations in that there will be a direct relationship between what children intend and what they express or produce. For example, a child may offer you a lump of playdough and ask you to taste their delicious cake – their symbolic representation is intended as a direct representation of their idea (even if the finished product is difficult to recognise as such). It is only later that second-order symbolism in the form of indirect symbols, such as letters and numbers, begins to emerge in their activities.

The case study below is an example of a child using a range of symbolic modes of representation to explore, express and communicate her thoughts about something that she had seen.

CASE STUDY

Young children representing thought

Sara, aged 3 years 10 months, had seen a hedgehog in her garden on the way to nursery. Her dad told the staff about it as he dropped her off. The practitioner asked Sara about the hedgehog but she was reluctant to say anything. Later on in the session, however, the practitioner noticed that in a number of ways Sara was exploring the experience of seeing the hedgehog and using the different materials and equipment available to communicate this experience.

First, she went over to the craft table and drew two slightly distorted semicircular shapes. She used the fat crayons available to do short spiky marks on each shape. On one she used blue, pink, yellow, green and orange and on the other a light orangey-brown. The many coloured hedgehog was done in larger, bolder more energetic strokes than the other one. The practitioner overheard Sara telling her friend that one was a good hedgehog and one was a bad hedgehog. She pointed to a series of vertical lines underneath each hedgehog, telling her friend that that says 'good hedgehog' and 'bad hedgehog'.

Later in the morning, Sara and a friend went over to the dressing-up area and emptied all the clothes out of the basket on to the floor then carefully put some of them back into the bottom of the basket to create a nest. Sara then curled up inside the basket and warned her friend, 'Don't stroke me because I am prickly.' Towards the end of the morning, Sara had made a clay hedgehog. It was a clay ball with matchsticks stuck into it. She brought it with her to listen to the story.

(Adapted from an idea in Kress, 1997)

The move into conventional literacy

As children continue to use a range of ways to communicate meaning and understanding in symbolic ways, and, given an appropriate range of experiences and opportunities with language and print, letters and numbers will begin to appear as part of their play and exploration. This is evidence of children's increasing awareness of print and its uses (*see* Chapter 6) and their growing conceptual understanding that print is a symbolic representation of speech. As Vygotsky (in Rieber and Hall, 1997, p142) observes, for children to move into becoming readers and writers they need to make a special discovery, that *not only things, but speech also can be drawn*. Children, he argues, must make the transition from drawing things to drawing words. This *special discovery* emerges from opportunities to engage with print (*see* Chapter 6) and to explore symbolic meaning making in substantial and sustained ways. Once children have shown that they have this understanding, the move into conventional literacy, including phonics, is then a small step forward from these firm foundations.

It is important to be aware that these are not strictly hierarchical developmental stages. There is an observable pattern and progression, but children will continue to use different modes to represent their understanding throughout childhood, including once they begin to learn phonics and read and write with reasonable proficiency. This would accord with the view of Kress (1997) that young children, in contrast to adults, tend to use the measure of *aptness* rather than convention, when selecting ways to represent their ideas.

DEVELOP YOUR UNDERSTANDING

Read through all the case studies and examples in *Mark Making Matters* (DCFS, 2008).

Make careful note of:

- the ways in which children represent their world symbolically through mark making;
- the meaning that the children ascribe to their marks;
- how letters and numbers emerge in children's representations of their world.

Please note that the EYFS has changed since the document was published but the examples of children's work are still very useful examples of symbol representation in children's mark-marking.

www.foundationyears.org.uk/wp-content/uploads/2011/10/Mark_Marking_Matters. pdf

---

Symbolic representation and children who are bilingual

In a series of studies, Bialystok (2001) concluded that young bilingual children had a more complete understanding of the symbolic relationship between print and meanings than monolingual children. This, she concludes, is because bilingual children acquire the cognitive insights essential for dealing with symbolic representations earlier than monolingual children. She argues that this may flow from their experience of oral language as the experience of managing two spoken systems has associated benefits of understanding the separation between form and meaning. This early understanding places these children in a privileged position as these insights are an important part of what leads into literacy. However, she warns that although these benefits are observable, there is no clearly understood direct route through to literacy, so these findings do not necessarily lead to the conclusion that there will be differences between bilingual and monolingual children in the rate or the manner in which they learn to read. Therefore, as parents and practitioners, what we need to know is that the same processes apply to both monolingual and bilingual children; they need opportunities for talking, book reading, play and mark making to enable them to develop an understanding of how to symbolise and represent their understanding symbolically.

Activities and experiences that support the ability to symbolise

To enable children to move towards becoming literate, including phonics, they need opportunities through interaction, play and with mark making to use gesture and items symbolically, and then to move towards representing their learning symbolically.

Initially, very young children need attentive and supportive adults who will tune into their attempts to communicate through gesture, as gesture is the early use of symbolic communication – using a movement or action to represent meaning. This may include, for example, waving, thumbs up, open hands for 'all gone'. Very young children need adults who will engage them in exchanges that involve gesture, and support and reinforce these early communicative interactions. These interactions happen as part of daily interaction where a young child uses symbolic gestures to communicate meaning in context and when needed for example: waving hello and goodbye as they arrive and leave; clapping to indicate something well done or to express appreciation. In addition, as children grow and learn, action rhymes are an excellent way to engage children in using gestures to symbolise meaning and linking gestures with another symbol that we use: language. The important thing is that, as parents and professionals working with young children, we are alive to the importance of gesture and engage with young children in the meanings they are communicating.

Learning to talk is also significant in the development of symbolic representation. Using words to represent people and objects is an early use of a symbol to represent something else. For example, a child's name is a spoken symbol for them. Children also come to recognise and use 'mummy' and 'daddy' (or an equivalent, or approximation) to represent particular people, and they begin to understand words that represent routines and activities in their lives, words such as drink, milk, dinner, bed or sleep. Parents and practitioners need to make sure that they use these words regularly and in context to enable children to make connections between person, event or routine and the word(s). Commentary is a useful interaction strategy to achieve this (*see* Chapter 3), as children will hear the word alongside what is happening or who is being referred to, and make connections between what they see and the symbol (word) used to represent it.

In addition to talking, children need to have the opportunity to hear storybooks read to them. This can start when children are very young as the more exposure they have to books and reading, the more likely they will develop the habit of reading. Having books read to them will enable children to come to know that the book carries a story, in both pictures and words. This early exposure to the representation of a story on the page is another way in which children absorb understandings about symbolic representation. This knowledge will initially be tacit, knowledge of which children are unaware. However, they will draw on this knowledge as they grow and learn more about symbolic representation, eventually drawing this into their conscious awareness when they begin to learn phonics and to read. Therefore, parents and practitioners need to read books to children and model reading as they do it. For example, pointing out the difference between pictures and print, drawing children's attention to the fact that both represent spoken words of the story, tracking the print, drawing children's attention to the symbols that represent the words, talking about letters and words, finding commonalities between symbols (letters, words) that are in the book and are important to them – for example their name, family members' names, etc.

As well as talking and reading with children, children need to play to develop their ability to symbolise. Play opens up opportunities for children to use things symbolically. Symbolic play (also referred to as pretend or imaginative play) is particularly valuable for developing this ability as it precipitates the transition from *things as objects of actions* to *things as objects of thought* (Fein, 1979, p4 in Stone and Stone, n.d., p3). This is because this type of play necessitates using one thing to represent another – for example, a box as a den, cones and stones as shopping, construction equipment as a wand or lightsaber.

All areas of play and provision in the home and in a setting have the possibility for pretending that involves children in symbolic play. It is observable that as children become involved in their play they often move into imaginative and pretend play – for example; jugs and containers in the water often become teapots and cups, and you are offered a cup of tea; playdough becomes a cake and you are offered a taste; a wooden structure in the outdoor area becomes a castle and you are ordered not to enter; and a big box becomes a dog kennel and you hear barking from inside. In all these examples of children's play, and many more, one of the things that children are learning, using and developing is the ability to symbolise – to use one thing to represent another.

Role play is a particularly good way for children to engage in symbolic play. When children engage in role play, alongside the props used, they are essentially using their body, voice and movements to represent someone else – for example, a mummy or a baby, a superhero, a doctor or vet, an animal or a story character. This will include a number of ways to represent the other person, the use of gesture and movement, a particular tone of voice or vocabulary, and/or the use of props and clothing to become someone else. Children therefore need to be offered opportunities that allow them to be imaginative and creative in role play. This is important. Children need the scope to imagine, as well as to replicate patterns of behaviour that they observe. So, for example, as well as providing costumes of known characters for children to dress up, provide clothing and fabric that they have to be creative with and use imaginatively to create a character or persona. Similarly, with provision for play as well as replicas of familiar items, provide more generic items that require children to imagine what they can be – for example, boxes, bowls and baskets, sticks and poles, pegs and fabric. There is also value in leaving children to seek out and develop their own imaginative play using what they can find, use and adapt in the environment to create an imaginative world. Again, the important thing is that as parents and professionals we understand the power of these play activities, and through our provision and interaction (and, at times, leaving them alone) enable and allow children to develop and sustain their play themes.

Alongside opportunities for children to engage in symbolic play, they also need opportunities for mark making. Mark making is another way in which children represent their world symbolically. This move into mark making is important as it begins the move from first-order symbolism to second-order symbolism. Initially, children's mark making will be focused on meaning making, representations of their feelings and experiences expressed through making marks. This may be in sand or foam or with water squirters, or in more conventional ways with paint, chalk or crayons. To begin with, children will often make marks without clear intent to represent something in particular so, although they may tell you what they have represented, this may shift and change in the telling. The purpose of this early mark making is often about expression and meaning making rather than accurate representation. A colleague of mine put this very succinctly: young children experience the act of painting before they paint what they experience.

With experience and maturation, children's mark making becomes more representative – what Vygotsky refers to as *drawing things*. This occurs prior to the appearance of letters and numbers in their mark making, which indicates a conceptual development into *drawing speech*. In settings, therefore, provision for children must include ample opportunities for mark making in different ways and on different scales. So we need to include the most obvious provision such as paper, card crayons, paint, etc. and opportunities to use these indoors and out, on a small and large scale, using a range of equipment. We also need to think beyond this and create other opportunities for mark making across the provision. For example: using touch screens; a tray or tough-spot full of sand, glitter or cornflour; wearing wellies to make marks in mud or snow; creating images and words with stones, feathers and twigs; using sweeping brushes in foam spread on the ground outside; driving wheeled vehicles through paint; providing equipment to squirt and pour water on to the ground and walls. Children also need the time and space to express, develop and consolidate their developing knowledge, understanding and skill. This means that our provision needs not only provide children with a range of activities, but also that they have opportunities to return to activities and repeat, extend and consolidate their developing skills. In addition, parents and practitioners need to mediate these experiences. For example, when appropriate and in context, encouraging children to talk about their marks and drawings; asking, noting and commenting on how they create meaning in their mark making and drawing; identifying and commenting on letters and numbers used in their mark making; modelling drawing and writing using commentary to communicate what you are doing.

Finally, in accordance with Vygotsky's notion of cultural tools, children need opportunities to engage with a range of other symbolic systems that we use: signs, symbols, maps, plans, numbers, musical notation, charts and models. Activities that enable children to represent things in these ways will need to be carefully considered to ensure that they are developmentally appropriate. For example, it is unlikely that children will be able to use conventional music notation. However, developmentally appropriate ways of recording musical ideas symbolically may include dots and dashes, lines and swirls, large and small strokes to indicate particular patterns of sound. What is important about these activities in the context of what comes before phonics is that all engagement in activities that encourage children to engage in symbolism will support their ability to represent their world symbolically which, in turn, creates firm foundations for later phonics teaching and learning.

Conclusion

This chapter has looked at what is meant by the ability to represent the world symbolically. It has explained the link between this and phonics teaching and learning. This issue has been considered for children who are bilingual. Examples have been given of interaction, activities and experiences that support children's ability to represent their world symbolically.

References

Bialystok, E (2001) *Bilingualism in Development: Language, Literacy and Cognition.* Cambridge: Cambridge University Press.

Bodrova, E and Leong, DJ (2015) Vygotskian and post-Vygotskian views on children's play. *American Journal of Play*, 7: 3 Available online at: **www.journalofplay.org/sites/www.journalofplay.org/files/pdf-articles/7-3-article-vygotskian-and-post-vygotskian-views.pdf** (accessed 11 September 2016).

DCFS (2008) Mark making matters. Available online at: **www.foundationyears.org.uk/wp-content/uploads/2011/10/Mark_Marking_Matters.pdf** (accessed 11 September 2016).

Kress, G (1997) *Before Writing: Rethinking Paths to Literacy.* London: Routledge.

Palmer, S (2005) The life of Vygotsky. Available online at: **www.suepalmer.co.uk/education_articles_lev_vygotsky.php** (accessed 11 September 2016).

Piaget, J and Inhelder, B (1972) *The Psychology of the Child.* New York: Basic Books.

Rieber, R and Hall, MJ (1997) *The Collected Works of LS Vygotsky: The History of the Development of Higher Mental Functions.* London: Plenum Press.

Stone, S and Stone, W (no date) Symbolic play and emergent literacy. Available online at: **www.iccp-play.org/documents/brno/stone1.pdf** (accessed 11 September 2016).

Vygotsky, L (1967) Play and its role in the mental development of the child. *Soviet Psychology*, 5: 6–18.

8 Phonological awareness

Introduction

Phonological awareness is the ability to focus on aspects of language other than their meaning – aspects of language such as rhyme, or clapping out syllables, or identifying words with the same initial sound. It also involves children becoming aware of letter-sound correspondence. Phonological awareness marks a transition into the earliest stages of phonics as children became sensitive to hearing and differentiating between sounds in words and language, prior to the more formal learning letter-sound correspondence for spelling and decoding.

This chapter explains what is meant by phonological awareness. It explores the relationship between phonological awareness and phonics, and outlines experiences and activities that develop phonological awareness.

As you read this chapter it is important to be aware that it is only an introduction to the topic of phonological awareness. This area of research is underpinned by *large, complex and seemingly contradictory literature on the associations between different*

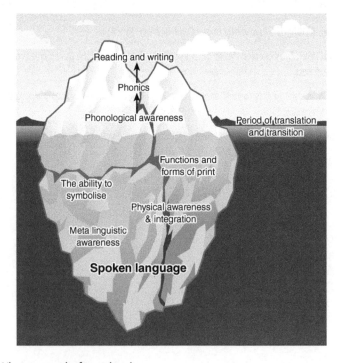

Figure 8.1 What comes before phonics

phonological skills and learning to read (Melby-Lervag *et al.*, 2012, p342). So, while the broad brushstrokes of our understanding of the relationship between phonological skills and learning to read are relatively clear and presented here in this chapter, there are still debates about the details of this relationship.

What is phonological awareness?

Phonological awareness refers to the ability to identify and manipulate units of oral language. This includes the ability to identify and make oral rhymes, and awareness of aspects of language such as words, syllables and onset–rimes. Children's ability to identify and manipulate oral language in these ways demonstrates a developing awareness of the detail within spoken language – the ability to focus on aspects of language beyond meaning.

In addition to identifying rhyme and the ability to separate language in words, syllables and onset–rime, a vital aspect of phonological awareness is the 'the ability to focus on and manipulate sounds (phonemes) in spoken words (National Reading Panel (NRP) 2000, p2.1). This is called phonemic awareness. Phonemic awareness is one part of the broader knowledge and skills that constitute phonological awareness, and usually appears after children are able to detect rhyme, and then identify and manipulate other aspects of language such as words, syllables and onset–rime.

The distinction between phonological awareness and phonics is important. Phonological awareness is the way in which children begin the process of hearing, identifying and manipulating oral aspects of language associated with sounds and letters (phonemes and graphemes) and sound-letter (phoneme–grapheme) correspondence. This oral ability to manipulate sounds leads into phonics which, in addition to continuing to develop children's oral abilities, also involves teaching children how to use grapheme–phoneme correspondence to decode and spell words (NRP, 2000, p2.2).

Understanding phonemes and graphemes

Phonemes are the smallest units constituting spoken language. English consists of about 44 phonemes. Phonemes combine to form syllables and words. A few words have only one phoneme, such as *a* or *oh*. Most words consist of a blend of phonemes, such as *at* with two phonemes (*a-t*), or *light* with three phonemes (*l-igh-t*), or *shut* with three phonemes (*sh-u-t*), or stand with five phonemes (*s-t-a-n-d*).

Phonemes are different from graphemes, which are units of written language and which represent phonemes in the spellings of words. Graphemes may consist of one letter – for example, *G-P-I-J-B-R* or multiple letters, *CH-SH-TH-CK-EA-IGH*, each symbolising one phoneme (NRP, 2000).

Phonological awareness: what comes before phonics?

There are a number of levels of language awareness as children begin to acquire pho-nological skills (Adams, 1990). To learn phonics to read and write, children need to shift their attention away from a single focus of comprehension of spoken language to a closer focus on individual words, syllables and phonemes. This requires that children refo-cus their attention from the level of comprehension of spoken language and focus on increasingly smaller units. Adams (1990) describes this as *pushing deeper into the system*, and notes that the deeper into the system they go, the more difficult it gets. Thus,

> *awareness of clauses or propositions develops earlier and more easily than awareness of words. Awareness of words develops earlier and more easily than awareness of syllables. And awareness of syllables develops earlier and more easily than awareness of phonemes.*

(Adams, 1990, p295)

Research shows that the acquisition of phonological awareness follows a sequential developmental pattern (Scharer and Zutell, 2013). This pattern has been shown to move from larger to smaller units in a stepwise pattern (Adams, 1990; Goswami, 2001):

- rhymes and alliteration;
- awareness of individual spoken words;
- syllables;
- onset–rime;
- phonemic awareness.

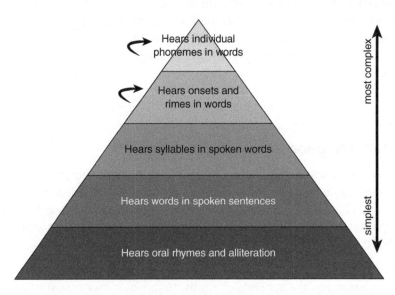

Figure 8.2   The acquisition of phonological awareness

Source: www.readingfirst.virginia.edu/prof_dev/phonemic_awareness/ri_phoneme.html (accessed 11 September 2016)

An important early aspect of phonological awareness is the ability to rhyme. Bryant *et al.*'s (1989) seminal work demonstrated that there was a relationship between very young children's knowledge of nursery rhymes and their later reading ability. They concluded that knowledge of nursery rhymes is related to the child's subsequent sensitivity to rhyme. This enhances children's phonological sensitivity, which in turn helps them to learn to read.

The importance of nursery rhymes (Bryant et al., 1989)

Bryant *et al.*'s (1989) study remains one of the most interesting and long-standing studies to make strong links between children's phonological skills and their later reading ability.

The study involved 64 children from a range of different backgrounds. The project was for three years. The children were aged from 2 years 10 months to 3 years 9 months at the beginning of the project, and from 5 years 9 months to 6 years 8 months at the end of the project. The research consisted of a parental questionnaire and a series of measures.

The research aimed to discover the relationship between four sets of measures taken over five sessions. The first two of these sessions were in the children's homes, and for the last three sessions the children were seen in their schools. The following four sets of measures were used.

1. *The children's knowledge of nursery rhymes*. Five of the most popular nursery rhymes were selected and children were asked if they could recite them and were recorded doing so. The five, chosen in a pilot study, were *Humpty Dumpty*, *Baa-Baa Black Sheep*, *Hickory Dickory Dock*, *Jack and Jill* and *Twinkle Twinkle Little Star*.

2. *Phonological sensitivity*. A series of tests were used to assess children's phonological sensitivity.

   Rhyme detection: These were used in the first two years. The children had to detect which words did not rhyme.

   Phoneme oddity: These tests were used in the third and fourth years. At 5 years 7 months children were asked to identify the first phoneme in words. At age 6 years 3 months they were asked to identify the final phoneme.

   Object naming: This was a non-phonological test related to reading ability used as a control test. This task has been shown to relate to reading ability. Children were shown a series of 10 pictures of familiar objects and asked to name them. They were timed on this task.

3. *Reading and spelling*. Spar reading tests A and B were completed at age 5 years 11 months (A) and 6 years 3 months (B). The SPAR spelling test was completed at age 5 years 11 months.

4. *IQ and vocabulary*. This was assessed using the standardised British Picture Vocabulary scale.

(Continued)

Bryant *et al*. (1989) conclude that:

> All in all, our results have shown a powerful and lasting connection between the children's early knowledge of nursery rhymes and aspects of their linguistic development later on. The nursery rhyme scores are connected to the development of phonological sensitivity over the next two to three years and, through that sensitivity, are linked to the children's success in learning to read and spell as well.

> (Bryant *et al*.,1989, p14, 426–7)

And comment that:

> The results of this study are particularly exciting because they show a strong link between an entirely informal experience early on in the child's life and a formal educational skill which the child must acquire some years later. When parents introduce their child to nursery rhymes it is most unlikely that eventual success in reading is in their minds. Yet our study makes it clear that this early knowledge of nursery rhymes may play a considerable role in preparing the child for reading and spelling.

> (Bryant *et al*., 1987, p425)

Words

In spoken interaction the natural focus of very young children's attention is on comprehension, making meaning from the combination of words in a speech stream. In the acquisition of phonological awareness, children's attention therefore needs to shift from a single focus on meaning to a broader focus that also attends to individual words. Adams (1990) comments that many young children do not readily understand the word 'word', but that knowing what a word is is essential to phonics and reading instruction. Therefore, to *make any sense whatsoever out of their classroom activities, children must already understand (or quickly catch on to) the idea of what a word is*. Ehri (1976) argues that one of the ways in which children learn about words is through exposure to print (*see* Chapter 6). She observes that when we speak, we speak in a speak stream, with no breaks or pauses between words and clauses. In contrast, print has a visual representation of individual words, and as they become aware of the one-by-oneness of words in print, they begin to notice and isolate words in speech.

Syllables

Syllables are deeper into the system than words. They are further removed from the meaning of language and nearer to phonemes (Adams, 1990). Unlike words, syllables are evident in the speech stream and research has shown that illiterate people can detect syllables in speech (Morais *et al*., 1986). Adams argues that attending to syllables is a rudimentary early developing skill that acts as an important mediator between children's attention to the sound structure of spoken language and its relationship to spelling, because syllabic awareness provides an essential link between the easy-to-acquire sensitivity to sound similarity and rhyme, and the hard-to-acquire capacity to recognise individual phonemes.

Onset–rime: between syllables and phonemes

Onset and rime refer to the two parts of a syllable, when it is divided into two. The onset consists of the consonants that precede the vowel. The rime consists of the vowel and any consonants that come after it – for example, *c-at*, *m-ail*, *fl-ag*, *tr-eat*. Adams (1990) observes that the capacity to attend to phonemes is not easily attained and that there is a big gap between syllables and phonemes, so awareness of onset–rime can act as an in-between stage, between syllables and phonemes. There are a number of reasons, including research outcomes, that point to the significance of onset–rime in phonological awareness. Adams, (1990) notes that onset–rime is a naturally felt division in words. She argues that there is naturalistic evidence that we rarely break onsets and rimes in our spoken language, and that we have a strong natural response to similarities in rime. Goswami's (1990, 2001) work concurs. She concluded that onset–rimes are particularly salient for young learners as their phonology becomes more segmented, and cites considerable evidence that this awareness of onset–rime predicts later success in reading and spelling.

What is onset–rime?

Onset: the phonological unit consisting of consonants that precede the vowel (not all words have onsets).

Rime: the phonological unit consisting of the vowel and any consonants that follow.

For example, dog = d-og = d (onset) og (rime); c-amp; b-ook; ph-one; j-ump; fr-og; sw-eet.

Phonemic awareness

To learn letter-sound correspondence, which is essential to learning to read, children must become aware of phonemes. Phonemes are the smallest units of sound in words (see definition in box on page 141). Phonemic awareness is the ability to hear, identify and orally manipulate phonemes in words. To acquire phonemic awareness, children need to become aware that phonemes exist as *abstractable and manipulable components of language* (Adams, 1990, p65). Phonemic awareness has been shown to be the most important prerequisite for learning to read (Melby-Lervag *et al.*, 2012; Adams, 1990). Adams (1990) observes that the extent to which children have learned to hear phonemes as individual and separate speech sounds will strengthen their ability to see individual letters and spelling patterns. And, conversely, the extent to which they have not learned to hear the phonemes will limit their ability. Adams refers to this as a *double or nothing return*. Melby-Lervag *et al.* (2012) conclude similarly. They conclude that the relationship between phonemic awareness and learning to read may be a causal one, in that adequate phonemic skill may be a prerequisite for learning to read effectively. In support of this, they observe that children who have difficulties with reading often show a deficit on phonemic awareness tasks and that there is strong evidence to suggest that *high-quality, phonically based reading instruction is effective in helping ameliorate children's word-level reading difficulties* (Melby-Lervag et al., 2012, p342).

Adams (1990) considers the issue of why phonemic awareness is relatively difficult to acquire. She notes that, as young children, we must 'know' about phonemes at some level to be able to produce and understand speech, and the errors and word play in spoken language – for example, recognising rhymes and alliterations, and in Spoonerisms in which we switch phonemes and morphemes in our speech (know your blows instead of blow your nose / flutter by instead of butterfly). Despite this, very young children's natural inclination is not to be consciously aware of phonemes, but to focus on fluency and meaning. To enable us to learn to speak fluently, we have had to free our minds of the detail of language and automate the process, sublimating our processing of phonemes to the capacity for understanding, fluency and meaning. Thus, the acquisition of phonemic awareness requires that children must learn to attend to attend to aspects of language that, in their spoken language, they have previously learned not to attend to.

This attention to the detail in language is vital in learning to read. As Adams (1990, p67) notes, research evidence shows children who are *low-readiness pre-readers* may well be able to hear the difference between phonemes but are unprepared to consciously analyse the sound structure of the syllables. Adams (1990, p65) concludes that the evidence points to the fact that it is not just working knowledge of phonemes that is important in learning to read, but conscious analytic knowledge. She notes that *it is neither the ability to hear the difference between two phonemes, nor the ability to distinctly produce them that is significant. What is important is the awareness that they exist as abstractable and manipulable components of the language*. And, vitally for early years practitioners and teachers, Adams (1990) concludes that the development of this capacity seems to depend on the encouragement to lend conscious attention to the sounds in words, as distinct from the meanings.

WHAT DOES RESEARCH TELL US?

Phonemic awareness (Adams, 1990)

There are a number of ways in which research has sought to understand the relationship between phonemic awareness and reading. Research studies have looked at young children's ability on phonemic awareness tasks, which is then mapped to their later ability in reading.

Adams (1990) outlines a range of tasks and tests that have sought to reveal the relationship between phonemic awareness and later ability in reading.

Phonemic segmentation tasks. These tasks are designed to see if children can segment a syllable into phonemes. In these tasks children are given a syllable and asked to tap out the phonemes or lay out counters or cards for each phoneme. Lieberman *et al.*'s

(Continued)

(1974) early use of these tests showed that the relationship between a tapping test and subsequent reading performance was strong. The strength of this relationship has been confirmed by later studies.

Phoneme manipulation tasks. In these tasks children are asked to manipulate the phonemes in a word in a particular way. For example, to pronounce a word after they have removed the first, middle or final phoneme (Bruce, 1964), so, *monkey* without the /m/ or *pink* without the /k/. Performance on these tests has yielded strong predictions or correlations with reading achievement.

Syllable-splitting tasks. In these tasks, children are asked to take off the first phoneme, then either say the word without the phoneme (researcher says 'cat', child responds 'at') or pronounce the phoneme in isolation (researcher says 'cat', child says 'c-c-c-c'). These tasks are more straightforward than phoneme segmentation or manipulation tasks. Children's success at these tasks has been shown to be strongly related to early reading acquisition.

Oddity tasks. In these tasks children are presented with a series of three or four spoken words and asked to identify which of the words is different or does not belong based on the first (*can, cake, pan*), last (*lend, send, sent*) or middle phoneme (*bun, sun, sat*).

The classic study in this area is Bryant and Bradley (1983) in which they found a highly significant relationship between children's oddity test scores and their later reading achievement. However, later studies by Bryant and Bradley were unable to answer precisely the question of whether it was phonemic awareness that caused differences in reading achievement or whether it was something more that they were unable to measure or control.

Adams (1990, p80) concludes that across the phonemic awareness tasks there are five levels of phonemic awareness:

1. Knowledge of rhyme; an ear for the sounds in words.

2. The ability to compare and contrast the sounds of words for rhyme and alliteration, evident in oddity tasks. This requires sensitivity to similarities and differences in the overall sound of words and the ability to focus on the components that make them similar or different.

3. Syllable splitting and blending. These require that children are familiar with the notion that words can be subdivided into small sounds (phonemes) and familiar with the sound and pronunciation of phonemes in isolation.

4. Phoneme segmentation. This requires that children have an understanding that words can be analysed into phonemes, and the ability to analyse them completely and on demand.

5. Phoneme manipulation. This requires further proficiency with the phonemic structure of words to be able to add, delete or move phonemes, and then regenerate a word or non-word.

(Continued)

147

WHAT DOES RESEARCH TELL US? *continued*

While all these tasks and tests have shown a strong relationship between phonemic awareness and later reading ability, some questions remain. For example, researchers question whether the skills and abilities demonstrated in the tasks actually test and demonstrate what they claim, whether or not the skills and abilities evident are transferable to the process of learning to read, and, perhaps most significantly, the direction of the relationship. Is phonemic awareness a prerequisite for early reading skills or do early reading skills enhance phonemic awareness, or is this relationship bidirectional? This issue is considered later in this chapter.

The relationship between phonological awareness, phonics and reading

Before the relationship between phonological awareness and phonics is discussed, it is important to reiterate the distinction between the two. Phonological awareness refers to the ability to hear, identify and manipulate syllables, onset–rime and phonemes in spoken language. Phonics continues this process and, in addition, involves the teaching of phoneme–grapheme correspondence.

The evidence for the necessity of having phonological awareness as a prerequisite for successfully accessing phonics is compelling: phonological awareness leads into phonics. The ability to hear and attend to rhymes, to recognise and identify a 'word', to segment words into syllables and onset–rime, provide a stepwise pattern of development that leads into the ability to segment words into their constituent phonemes. The acquisition of phonological awareness is the move from being able to identify and manipulate the large unit of a 'word' to the small unit of phonemes (phonemic awareness).

The final stage of this process is that this oral ability with phonemes must be linked with letters (graphemes) to enable children to read and write. This is phonics. The evidence is clear that children with good phonemic awareness are likely to come to phonics teaching with a high chance of success, linking their orally articulated knowledge of sounds to the corresponding grapheme. Clearly, this is not a guarantee but good phonemic awareness is very likely to yield dividends in the acquisition of reading skills (NRP, 2000, pp2–7).

While the development of phonological awareness is presented here as a neat step-wise developmental trajectory, it is unlikely to be as neat and straightforward in reality. Within the development of phonological awareness, the move is highly likely to be from large units to small units in language (words–phonemes), but children will respond in different ways to different things, so the pace, timing, flow and emphasis within children's phonological development will differ. For example, some children may respond well to a focus on onset–rime, while others may find that developing the concept of a word takes some time; some children will move very quickly to developing phonemic awareness, while others may make slow but steady progress through all the identified aspects of phonological awareness.

There is also a question of directionality in the process of acquiring phonological awareness: is it a hierarchical process in which one aspect of phonological aware-ness necessarily precedes another, or is the relationship between the different aspects more complex than that?

Directionality

Adams (1990, p331) concludes that phonological awareness develops in a step-wise pattern from large units to small units prior to the development of phonemic awareness. Thus, children move from the ability to hear rhyme and alliteration to understanding the concept of a word through the ability to break words into sylla-bles and onset–rime. The relationship then becomes bidirectional in that there is a mutually positive relationship between learning to read and developing phonemic awareness. Therefore, once you are in the process of developing phonemic aware-ness, it is easier to learn to read, and learning to read develops phonemic awareness. Melby-Levag *et al*. (2012, p342) concur, noting that despite their conclusion that pho-nemic awareness is a causal influence on word reading skills, this does not discount the reciprocal relationship between word reading and phonemic awareness (see research on pages 154–5).

What this leads to is the conclusion that the initial development through phonologi-cal awareness to phonemic awareness is vital. Children need phonological awareness (including phonemic awareness) prior to learning phonics and progressing on to reading and writing. They need opportunities and adult mediation to support the progressive development of phonological awareness through to the oral ability to identify phonemes because, once children have phonemic awareness, the move into phonics is a small next step. And, as Adams (1990) and Melby-Levag *et al*. (2012) observe, this then becomes a reciprocal relationship in which phonemic awareness supports phonics and learning to read, and phonics and learning to read support phonemic awareness. This mutually supportive relationship has parallels with the Matthew effect in reading (*see* Chapter 2). The Matthew effect states that the devel-opment of reading is supported by reading, thus children who can read get better at reading by reading. In the same way, using phonemic awareness skills when learning to read supports phonemic awareness skills. Developing good phonological aware-ness through to phonemic awareness is therefore vital in anticipation of children successfully learning to read.

Activities and experiences that develop phonological awareness

For children to develop phonological awareness, they need a range of opportunities and activities that are provided by, and mediated by, adults. These opportunities need to be mapped to children's developing abilities. This is important to ensure that children are not moved on before their understanding is secure, or that they are not held back when they have demonstrated secure knowledge in advance of expectations.

Effective pedagogy to support young children's phonological development is focused on weaving learning into activities, experiences and routines by being aware of opportunities that arise to develop children's phonological awareness. This approach is developmentally appropriate and contextualises children's learning in a meaningful way. There is likely to be a shift in pedagogical approach in the later stages of phonemic awareness as evidence suggests that some explicit teaching of phonemic awareness is useful. All of this requires that practitioners and teachers have a good understanding of phonological awareness, of the potential of activities and interaction to support this, and appropriate pedagogical strategies that are mapped to children's developing needs.

Hearing and responding to sound, rhyme and alliteration

The earliest aspect of phonological awareness is the ability to hear rhymes and alliteration. Therefore, from being a baby, children need the opportunity to engage with rhymes, songs and poems to 'tune' their ear into the sound of rhyme and alliteration. This needs to continue and increase through early childhood with the rhymes etc. becoming increasingly sophisticated, and children being encouraged to think and talk about the rhymes and alliteration.

Language play will also encourage and develop sensitivity to rhyme and alliteration. Given the opportunity, children love to mess around with language, to make nonsense rhymes, and continue strings of alliterative, rhyming and non-rhyming words, often just for the pleasure of producing and hearing language.

Many storybooks for young children have a rhyming scheme, or alliterative sections, and children will quickly pick up the rhyme and cadence and join in. As Adams (1990) notes, we all appear to have a natural affinity for rhyme. Children will eventually be able to anticipate the rhyming scheme and alliterative sentences and join in. Again, playing with the language in these books by changing words, or initial sounds, or by continuing rhyming and alliterative strings will draw children's attention to rhyme and alliteration in language, and offer early opportunities for children to manipulate language.

These opportunities to hear and interact with rhymes, songs, poems and books, and to engage in language play have the additional benefit of drawing children's attention to words. One part of phonological awareness is the ability to perceive a word as a separate unit and, as Adams notes, this means shifting children's attention to noticing this aspect of language alongside their strong, natural focus on meaning-making in language. These early opportunities to focus on words begin this process.

In addition to specific awareness of rhyme and alliteration, young children need opportunities to listen and respond to a wide range of sound prior to being introduced to letter sounds. This includes music, environmental sounds and interpreting sound through movement. Children need opportunities to tune into sounds, to develop sensitivity to what they hear, to begin to discriminate between sounds, and to respond to and talk about what they hear. All of this anticipates phonological awareness, which can include the following.

- Actively listening to music. Create time to listen to music, which could be when travelling, resting, eating or doing an activity. Offer a range of music to listen to – music from TV programmes and popular films, popular and classical music. Encourage children to listen to the music, and use commentary and discussion to begin to describe what you have heard.

- Making music using opportunities in the environment, body percussion and percussion instruments. These opportunities can be provided indoors and outdoors, done informally or in groups, adult-led or child-directed. The important aspect of this in relation to phonological awareness is that children are making, listening to and manipulating sounds.

- Physical movement and dance. Encourage children to listen carefully and respond physically to the music. Is it music that makes you want to sway, or jump up and down, or stamp, swirl, to move quickly or slowly? Movement and dance can be combined with language using rhymes and alliterative strings – for example, stomp-stomp-stomp-stomp-tiptoe-tiptoe-tiptoe-tiptoe-stomp-stomp tiptoe-tiptoe-stomp-stomp-tiptoe-tiptoe-stomp-stomp-stop!

- Stories with sound effects. Choose a story that could involve sound effects, and work together at adding sound effects at the appropriate moment. For example, in *The Gruffalo* (Donaldson, 1999), one of the sound effects could be for the mouse walking through the wood, another for the appearance of the Gruffalo, different ones for terrible teeth and terrible claws, one for his turned out knees, his poisonous wart and his purple prickles, and each time this occurs in the story the appropriate sound effect is used.

- Listening to stories. In addition to reading storybooks, provide opportunities for children to listen to stories, perhaps on CDs or tablets, or even a book without showing children the pictures. Removing the visual cues means that they need to listen carefully to the story. Clearly, the length and complexity of the storyline will need to be matched to the children's abilities.

- Drawing children's attention to sounds in the environment, and labelling and talking about what you hear – aircraft, trucks, trains, wind, dogs barking, trees moving.

- Making sound in the environment: using movement and opportunities that arise to make and enjoy sounds in the indoor and outdoor environment; knocking, banging, rubbing, rattling, shaking, dropping, pulling and pushing. Draw children's attention to, and talk about, the sounds that they are making.

- Play listening games. Table-top/tablet-based games that encourage careful listening, such as sound bingo. Play games such as musical statues or sleeping lions in which children have to listen and respond.

Phase one of the DFE (2007) guidance *Letters and Sounds* has a range of ideas for practitioners in settings to support these early listening and attending skills. Similar to the ideas above, they encourage staff to develop children's ability to listen carefully and respond to sound, and to begin to think about and make sounds. At phase one the activities they suggest are designed to develop the following skills:

- tuning into sounds;

- listening and remembering sounds;

- talking about sounds.

There is a range of games and activities outlined in the guidance designed to develop these earlier phonological skills.

Segmenting words: syllables, onset–rime and phonemes

Early experiences with listening, responding and manipulating sound anticipates the move into segmenting words and phonemic awareness. However, as Adams (1990) notes, progression through to the acquisition of phonemic awareness is not triggered by mere exposure to language. Unlike sensitivity to rhyming, which children seem to have naturally, attending to smaller units of language requires mediation. Children need to be encouraged to notice and attend to increasingly smaller units such as syllables, onset–rime and phonemes. This is important. Both parents and practitioners need to draw children's attention to the ways in which we can divide up words into smaller units, including phonemes. There are plenty of opportunities in daily interaction and routines, as well as in activities, to achieve this. An informal, naturalistic and contextualised approach is an appropriate pedagogical approach for young children to develop phonological awareness. Some examples of this approach are as follows.

- Point out words in environmental print, on packaging, clothing, toys, logos and signs etc. This approach with environmental print can be developed, segmenting words into syllables, onset–rimes or phonemes, or by drawing children's attention to similarities between phonemes such as an initial phoneme in a logo that is the same initial phoneme as their name.

- In settings, daily routines and interactions provide opportunities for children's attention to be drawn to words and phonemes, for example:

  o pointing out the word that says a child's name on name labels;

  o orally segmenting a child's name into syllables, onset–rime or phonemes;

  o as a way of organisation – for example, 'all children with an s-s-s-s at the beginning of their name can get their coat';

  o sounding out phonetically regular words when reading books, instructions, or environmental point;

  o identifying phonemes and segmenting words into syllables, onset–rime and/or phonemes when modelling writing;

  o identifying the phonemes in the rhyme or alliteration in rhymes, poems, songs, and books.

- Language play in everyday interactions is another way to tune children into hearing words segmented, including into phonemes – for example, tapping or clapping the syllables when asking children to do things; making silly sentences by separating words into onset–rime – for example, *T-ime t-o p-ut y-our c-oat o-n;* to identify phonemes, *Guess what we are going to have to eat? ... it begins with p-p-p-p-p ... it's pizza!* Children will quickly catch on to these interactions and have a go. Initially, they may not hear the syllables or phoneme and make random attempts or guesses but, as with all learning, children need lots of modelling and repetition to enable them to learn.

Finally, once children have a strong foundation on which to build phonemic awareness, more activities explicitly focused on learning phonemes can form part of their experience. As Adams (1990, p331) notes, *towards the goal of efficient and effective reading instruction the explicit teaching of phonemic awareness is invaluable*. This more explicit teaching should be play based and enjoyable as children need to experience a significant degree of success in these early attempts with oral recognition of phonemes. This is to ensure that children feel competent and are motivated to continue as the acquisition of phonemic awareness is not easy and will require significant persistence. Pedagogically, the aim is to build the teaching of phonemes into play-based familiar activities rather than move to a pedagogy based on more formal teacher-led school type activities. Developmentally appropriate pedagogy could include activities such as the following.

- Group games focused on hearing and identifying particular phonemes, such as feely bags, parachute games and ring games.

- Tablet, white board and electronic toy-based activities and games focused on oral recognition of phonemes.

- Sound walks, indoors and outdoors; identifying, collecting or taking photos of items on a walk that begin with a particular phoneme(s).

- A treasure hunt: in the sand, or hidden around the nursery indoors or outdoors; buried or hidden items that children have to find and orally identify the initial sound. Collect items that begin with the same initial phoneme in treasure boxes.

- Combining physical activity with oral articulation of phonemes – for example, bouncing a ball while saying *b-b-b-b-b-ball*. Rolling along the ground *r-r-r-r-roll*. Jumping up and down *j-j-j-j-j jump*. Sliding *s-s-s-s-slide*. Hopping *h-h-h-h-hop*.

In line with Adams's assertion and the developmental trajectory within phonological awareness, the final stage of phase one of *Letters and Sounds* (DFE, 2007) is oral blending and segmenting. Again, the guidance identifies a range of activities and interactions to support children's development.

What is significant in the context of what comes before phonics is that prior to the beginning of this more focused teaching of phonemic awareness, children have a firm foundation of the range of knowledge and skills identified in this chapter to enable them to access this teaching with a high chance of success.

Phonological skills and their role in learning to read: a meta-analytic review (Melby-Lervag et al., 2012)

Melby-Lervag *et al.* (2012) conducted a systematic meta-analytic review of phonological skills and their role in learning to read.

A systematic meta-analytic review is a research method that seeks to answer a question by gathering and analysing existing research evidence within a particular area. A systematic review seeks to answer a defined research question by collecting and summarising all empirical evidence that fits pre-specified eligibility criteria, and a meta-analysis is the use of statistical methods to summarise the results of these studies (CCACE, 2013).

Melby-Levag *et al.* (2012) argue that there is a need for such a review of the existing evidence, as authors of previous research have claimed a potential causal link between phonological ability, phonemic awareness, rime awareness and verbal short-term memory and the development of children's word reading skill. Their intention, therefore, was to look across existing research evidence to seek to establish the strength of the relationship between each of these measures and children's word reading skills. Their research began with three hypotheses that they wished to test in the meta-analysis (Melby-Levag *et al.*, 2012, p327).

Hypothesis one. Phonemic awareness, rime awareness and verbal short-term memory will be significant correlates of individual differences in children's word reading skills.

Hypothesis two. Of these three predictors, phonemic awareness will be most closely associated with individual differences in children's word reading skills.

Hypothesis three. Only phonemic awareness will be an independent predictor of individual differences in children's word reading skills.

The results from the meta-analysis provided clear support for all three hypotheses.

1. Phonemic awareness, rime and non-verbal short-term memory are reliable correlates of individual differences in children's word reading skills.

2. Of these three correlates, phonemic awareness showed the strongest correlation with individual differences in children's word reading skills.

3. Only phonemic awareness is a unique predictor of individual differences in children's word reading skills.

The team concluded that

There is a specific and substantial association between concurrent measures of phonemic awareness and children's word reading skills. In contrast, rime awareness and verbal short-term memory are significantly weaker correlates of children's word reading skills.

(p340)

(Continued)

154

WHAT DOES RESEARCH TELL US? *continued*

In addition, and very importantly, Melby-Levag *et al*. (2012, p341) argue that the pattern which is evident in the meta-analysis, combined with evidence from longitudinal and training studies, leads them to conclude that *phonemic awareness is likely to be one causal influence on the development of word reading skills*. Thus, *phonemic skills are one critical determinant of success in learning to read* (p342).

NB Correlation and causation are important terms to understand. They are often used incorrectly.

- A correlation means that there is a relationship or connection between two or more things. One *doesn't* cause the other, but there is a noted relationship between things.

- Causation means that one thing causes another; there is the production of an effect by the cause.

DEVELOP YOUR UNDERSTANDING

Phonological awareness, including phonemic awareness, is vital for learning phonics.

- It is therefore equally vital that early years staff have a good understanding of both phonological and phonemic awareness.

- It is also vital that early years staff know how to support children's learning in this area, so that provision and interaction are well focused and developmentally appropriate.

- Provision that is informed by this professional knowledge and understanding will enable children to come later to phonics teaching with a high chance of success.

Make sure that you have a strong professional understanding of phonological awareness and appropriate pedagogical approaches to support young children's learning in this area of literacy.

Read back through this chapter which has covered the basics of the topic. The reference list at the end of the chapter provides some good starting points for deepening your understanding.

Conclusion

This chapter has explained what is meant by phonological awareness. It has outlined each *aspect* of phonological awareness. The relationship between phonological awareness and phonics has been considered, emphasising the importance of phonological awareness in becoming literate. Experiences, activities and pedagogical approaches that support children's developing phonological awareness have been identified.

References

Adams, MJ (1990) *Beginning to Read: Thinking and Learning About Print.* London: MIT Press.

Bruce, LJ (1964) In Adams, MJ (1990) *Beginning to Read: Thinking and Learning About Print.* London: MIT Press.

Bryant, PE, Bradley, L (1983) In Adams, MJ (1990) *Beginning to Read: Thinking and Learning About Print.* London: MIT Press.

Bryant, PE, Bradley, L, Maclean, M and Crossland, J (1989) Nursery rhymes, phonological skills and reading. *Journal of Child Language,* 16(2): 407–28.

CCACE (2013) Systematic reviews and meta-analyses: A step-by-step guide. Available online at: **www.ccace.ed.ac.uk/research/software-resources/systematic-reviews-and-meta-analyses** (accessed 11 September 2016).

DFE (2007) Letters and sounds: Principles and practice of high quality phonics. Available online at: **www.gov.uk/government/uploads/system/uploads/attachment_data/file/190599/Letters_and_Sounds_-_DFES-00281-2007.pdf** (accessed 11 September 2016).

Donaldson, J (1999) *The Gruffalo.* London: Macmillan.

Ehri, LC (1976) in Adams, MJ (1990) *Beginning to Read: Thinking and Learning About Print.* London: MIT Press.

Goswami, U (2001) in Scharer, P *The Sage Handbook of Early Childhood Literacy.* London: SAGE.

Scharer, PL and Zutell, J (2013) The Development of Spelling. In Larson, J and Marsh, J (2013) (eds).

Goswami, U and Bryant, P (1990) *Phonological Skills and Learning to Read.* Hove: Psychology Press

Lieberman, IJ, Shankweiler, D, Fischer, FW and Carter, B (1974) In Adams, MJ (1990) *Beginning to Read: Thinking and Learning About Print.* London: MIT Press.

Melby-Lervag, M, Lyster, SA and Hulme, C (2012) Phonological skills and their role in learning to read: A meta-analytic review. *Psychological Bulletin,* 138(2): 322–52.

Morais, J, Bertelson, P, Cary, L and Alegria, J (1986) in Adams, MJ (1990) *Beginning to Read: Thinking and Learning About Print.* London: MIT Press.

National Reading Panel (NRP) (2000) Teaching children to read. Available at: **www.nichd.nih.gov/publications/pubs/nrp/documents/report.pdf** (accessed 11 September 2016).

Scharer, PL and Zutell, J (2013) The development of spelling. In Larson, J and Marsh, J (2013) (eds) *The SAGE Handbook of Early Childhood Literacy.* London: Sage.

Conclusion

Becoming literate

Becoming literate is essential to children's learning at school and beyond and there is thus an emphasis on literacy in early years and school. Research evidence shows that phonics is an important part of becoming literate (Torgerson *et al.*, 2006), and therefore, this has become a strong focus in early literacy teaching (DFE, 2013). Research evidence indicates that although phonics is necessary to become literate, it is insufficient on its own to enable children to read (and write) with understanding and enjoyment (Torgerson *et al.*, 2006). We know that to be effective, phonics teaching needs to be embedded in a rich literacy environment (EEF, 2015). Evidence shows that this is also the case for children who are learning English as an additional language (Burgoyne *et al.*, 2011).

As phonics is necessary to become literate, it is important that young children come to phonics with the knowledge and skill that will enable them to access the teaching easily and with a high chance of success. For children to be able to do this, they need to have had learning experiences in their early years that lay the important foundations for becoming literate, including learning phonics (EEF, 2015; NICHD, 2006; Clay, 1991; Adams, 1990).

However, despite this strong consensus about the importance of phonics in becoming literate, there are ongoing concerns about the appropriateness of the current approach to literacy teaching and learning for very young children (Flewitt, 2014; Goouch and Lambrith, 2011; House, 2011). This includes concern about the appropriateness of early, formal teaching, including the teaching of phonics. It is argued that it is pedagogically inappropriate for many young children, and because it is *too much too soon* (House, 2011), children are being introduced to concepts through formal teaching before they have had sufficient opportunity to develop necessary underpinning knowledge and skill.

In terms of phonics, this is compounded by the fact that while there is a significant body of literature and initial and continuing professional development opportunities for teachers and practitioners to become proficient in teaching phonics, there are far fewer opportunities to become knowledgeable about what comes before phonics. Therefore, to address these concerns, and to ensure that strong professional knowledge underpins our work in early years, we need to be clear about what we should be focusing on in a child's earliest years. What do children need to know and experience to enable them to access later phonics teaching with success?

What comes before phonics?

Reading and writing are the visible products of being literate. Learning to read and write is supported by knowledge, understandings, skills and attitudes that are learned and developed in a child's earliest years. A good analogy for this is an iceberg. In this analogy, the visible tip represents the visible skills of reading and writing. This is supported by what lies underneath: far less visible, but absolutely necessary.

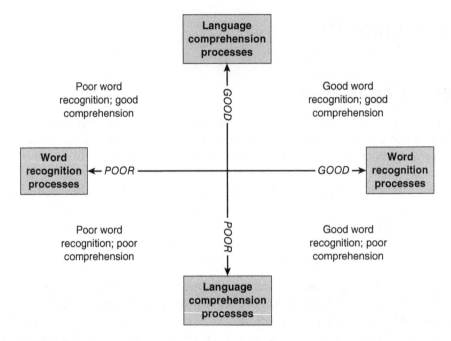

Image 1.2(a)

This analogy is the same for phonics. The visible acquisition of phonics is similarly underpinned by a range of knowledge, understandings, skills and attitudes. These are learned and developed in early childhood, and increase the likelihood of young children coming to phonics teaching ready to learn and with a high chance of success.

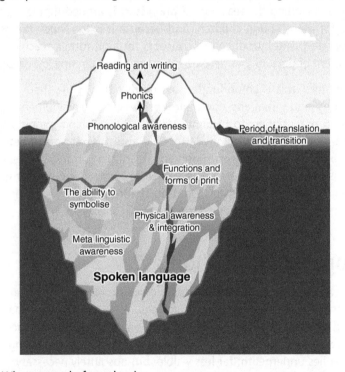

Figure C.1 What comes before phonics

The necessary knowledge and skills have been outlined in detail in the book chapters. In summary, they include the following.

- *Spoken language*. Spoken language, and the ability to listen carefully and respond, are the foundation on which later teaching and learning, including phonics, are built. Children learn language. To achieve this they need rich language experiences that include adults who say more than is necessary, opportunities for silence and careful listening, and play and interaction that enables them to engage in talk.

- *Physical activity that supports sensory awareness and integration*. Physical development is integral to learning. Children need to develop a range of physical skills to enable them to engage effectively in learning, and to be able to sit still and focus. This includes balance and proprioception, crossing the midline, and sensory awareness and integration. These skills are not developed by sitting still. Young children need to move and be active to develop these physical foundations for learning.

- *Meta-linguistic awareness*. To access phonics teaching with success children need to be able to think and talk about language. This is called metalinguistic knowledge. Young children need to become aware of language as an object that is composed of words and meanings that can be examined, discussed and manipulated. This can be achieved in the ways in which we interact with children, through language play and through reading storybooks.

- *An understanding of the functions and forms of print.* Becoming literate needs a context. Children need to develop an understanding of why, where and how print (including digital print) is used, so that learning phonics and to read and write are meaningful activities. Children are surrounded by literacy and come to know about the functions and forms of print through engagement with print in their everyday lives and in their play. Adults need to mediate this engagement to support children's emerging understanding, and use, of print.

- *The ability to symbolise*. The ability to use one thing to represent another is fundamental to literacy. Writing is the symbolic representation of speech and reading is the decoding of symbols. Phonics is therefore the symbolic basis of our system of reading and writing. Learning to symbolise requires that children make the cognitive shift from first- to second-order symbolism. This is achieved through children's use of gesture and language, through symbolic use of resources in their play and, eventually, in their mark marking. As Vygotsky (1967, p12) notes, *at the critical moment when a stick (an object) becomes a pivot for severing the meaning of 'horse' from a real horse the basic psychological structures for determining the child's relationship to reality is radically altered.*

- *Phonological awareness*. The acquisition of phonological awareness marks a child's earliest move into more formal aspects of learning phonics. Phonological awareness is the ability to identify and orally manipulate units of language, such as identifying oral rhymes, and an awareness of aspects of language such as words, syllables and onset–rime. The final stage of phonological awareness is phonemic awareness. This is the ability to hear, identify and orally manipulate phonemes.

The acquisition of phonemic awareness has been shown to be causally linked to later phonics learning (Melby-Lervag *et al.*, 2012). To achieve this, children need adults to focus and mediate their learning. This requires adults to weave learning into activities, experiences and routines by being aware of, and exploiting, opportunities to develop these skills within meaningful contexts. There is likely to be a shift in this pedagogical approach as children move into acquiring phonemic awareness, as evidence suggests that some explicit teaching of this is useful. Phonics teaching then continues this oral process and, in addition, involves the teaching of phoneme–grapheme correspondence.

Brought together, this knowledge, skill and understanding create a framework for what comes before phonics. It is not a prescribed set of outcomes, but a way of articulating and framing what is known about early experiences that enable children to come to phonics teaching with a good chance of success.

Professional knowledge

This professional knowledge and understanding is vital for effective literacy teaching in the early years. Clearly, the emphasis on phonics in settings and schools is an important aspect of becoming literate, so it follows that early years provision and pedagogy should ensure that when they come to it, children are able to access the teaching with ease, and with a high chance of success. It is therefore an essential part of early years professional knowledge that we understand, and have the pedagogical skill, to provide developmentally appropriate opportunities and experiences that lead into phonics.

This framework provides a basis for understanding and providing for developmentally appropriate early literacy teaching and learning. It enables us to articulate and defend an approach to literacy that acknowledges the importance of phonics in becoming literate within a pedagogical approach that is based on what is known about how young children learn, and about what comes before phonics.

We all share the aim of enabling children to become literate with ease and success. However, as Camus (in Neaum, 2016) argues, *Good intentions can do as much harm as malevolence if they lack understanding.*

References

Adams, MJ (1990) *Beginning to Read: Thinking and Learning About Print.* London: MIT Press.

Burgoyne, K, Whiteley, HE and Hutchinson, JM (2011) The development of comprehension and reading-related skills in children learning English as an additional language and their monolingual, English-speaking peers. *British Journal of Educational Psychology,* 81(2): 344–54.

Clay, M (1990) *Becoming Literate: The Construction of Inner Control.* London: Heinemann.

DFE (2013) Early Years Outcomes. Available online at: **www.foundationyears.org.uk/files/2012/03/Early_Years_Outcomes.pdf** (accessed 11 September 2016).

EEF (Education Endowment Foundation) (2015) Phonics. Available online at: **https://educationendowmentfoundation.org.uk/ evidence/teaching-learning-toolkit/phonics/** (accessed 11 September 2016).

Flewitt, R (2014) Early Literacy Learning in the Contemporary Age. In Moyles, J, Georgeson, J and Payler, J (eds) (2014) *Early Years Foundations: Critical Issues* (2nd edn). Berkshire: Oxford University Press.

Goouch, C and Lambrith, A (2011) *Teaching Early Reading and Phonics*. London: SAGE.

House, R (ed.) (2011) *Too Much, Too Soon? Early Learning and the Erosion of Childhood.* Gloucester: Hawthorne Press.

Melby-Lervåg, M, Lyster, S and Hulme, C (2012) Phonological skills and their role in learning to read: A meta-analytic review. *Psychological Bulletin*, 138(2): 322–52.

Neaum, S (2016) School readiness and the pedagogies of Competence and Performance. *International Journal of Early Years Education*, 24(3): 239–53.

NICHD (2006) Teaching children to read: Report of the National Reading Panel: Findings and determinations. Available online at: **www. nichd.nih.gov/publications/pubs/nrp/documents/report.pdf** (accessed 11 September 2016).

Torgerson, C, Brooks, G and Hall, J (2006) A systematic review of the research literature on the use of phonics in the teaching of reading and spelling. Available online at: **http://dera.ioe.ac.uk/14791/1/RR711_.pdf** (accessed 11 September 2016).

Vygotsky (1967) Play and its role in the mental development of the child. *Soviet Psychology*, 5: 6–18.

Index

activities, physical as literacy 87
adult-focused activities 45 (study)
  in setting 43
agency in play (study) 45
aim of book 8
alliteration and phonological awareness 150
ambiguity and comprehension of text 101–2
attachment, bonds of 54
augmentative communication, benefits of 41

babies:
  physical development opportunities 84–6
  sensory stimulation 86
babies, talking with 65–7
  contingency 66
  in day-care 67
  effective interaction 66–7
  gesture 66
  strategies for 65–7
balance and learning 75–6
Behaviourism 50–1
  limitations 51
bilateral coordination, stages in 77
bilingual children:
  advantages for 6
  English language learning support
    techniques 65
  and monolingual compared 103, 135
  and print awareness 113–14
  and symbolic representation 135
bilingualism:
  background variability 57
  and metalinguistic knowledge 102–3
body and mind connections 76
books and comprehension 68–9
brain architecture 36–7
  early years' importance 37
  and experiences 36
Bronfenbrenner, Urie, learning theories 52
Bruner on language learning 53–4

child-initiated play:
  research 44
  in setting 43
choice, repertoires of (study) 46
Chomsky, Noam on language learning 51–2
commentary in interaction 62
communication:
  language for 52
  tools for 52
Communication Friendly Spaces 64–5
competent social actors 44
comprehension:
  of ambiguous text 101–2
  and books, rhymes and songs 68–9

consequences of literacy 1–2
context of literacy, current 11–28
control and metalinguistic knowledge
    bidirectionality 96
crawling, benefits of 85
curriculum-focused or child-focused
    provision 87

dance and phonological awareness 151
day-care:
  interaction with babies in 67
  literate environment 67
developmental theories 25
developmentalism in emergent literacy 121
digital environment, print in 109–10
digital literacy 109–10
directionality of learning 96

EAL see English as additional language
early learning, views of 24
early readers, linguistic environment of (study)
    60–1
early years:
  merging with school 26
  as preparation for school 25
  provision supporting literacy learning 37–43
  and school 25–6
educational failure, factors in 77
effective reading:
  and language comprehension 101
  and word reading 101
elaborated talking 66–7
emergent comprehension 31
emergent literacy 31–7
  at home 33, 114–16
  and environmental print (study) 107–8
  justification for term 112–13
  and later learning 35
  mediation of experiences 115–16
  modelling behaviours 115
  parental involvement 125–6
  patterns of organisation 115
  pedagogy of 120–1
  practices (study) 31–3
  scaffolding skills at home (study) 116–18
  in settings 119–25
  stages of 121
emergent reading:
  encouraging 115–16
  stages of 122
emergent writing 123–4 (table), 124–5 (study)
  encouraging 116
  levels of understanding in 122–3
  non-linear process 125
employment, education for 18

engaging with literacy day-to-day 30–1
English as additional language:
  advantages 6
  comprehension of text 17
  inclusion 41
  numbers of children with 5–6
  phonics necessary but not sufficient 6
  process of learning phonics 17
  stages of learning 58–9
  supporting learning 65
environment for literacy 40
environmental print 107, 125
  and emergent literacy (review) 107–8
  encouragement of understanding 115
  guided exposure to 117–18
  parental involvement 125
epi-linguistic control 94
eye-tracking 81

Foundation Stage, teaching reading current
    approach 11–18
free play, choices in (study) 45
frustration, resolution of in play (study) 46

gesture:
  and language acquisition 54–5
  symbolic representation 136
grammar in language learning 53
graphemes:
  meaning 141
  and phonemes linking 148

home:
  emergent literacy in 33, 114–16
  learning environment 69
  and literacy learning 30–7

inclusion in play activities 45 (study)
intention reading in language acquisition 53
interaction in language acquisition 60–9
iPads:
  print awareness and 109–10
  writing supported by 109, 110

jokes and metalinguistic awareness 99–100

Key Stage 1, teaching reading current approach
  11–18

language:
  development 49–72
  features highlighted 97
  for language 97
  precursors 54–5
  as social process 51–2
  and thought 52
language acquisition 49–72
  family talk influences 55–6
  innate capacity 55
  interaction in 60–9

language acquisition *cont.*
  listening in 59
  silence in 59
  social interaction (study) 55–6
  theories 50–4
Language Acquisition Device (Chomsky) 51
Language Acquisition Support System (Bruner) 52–3
language awareness:
  and language comprehension 100
  levels of 142
language comprehension:
  components of 101
  and effective reading 101
  and language awareness 100
  mental model of text 101
  in Simple View of Reading 14–15
language learning:
  parental involvement methods 70
  reinforcement in 50
  social interaction 55
language play:
  and language development 68
  and phonemic awareness 153
  and phonological awareness 150
learning environment, coercive power of (study)
  119–20
listening:
  carefully by practitioners 63
  in language acquisition 59
  and literacy 38–9
  and phonological awareness 151
literacy:
  antecedents (study) 98
  consequences 1–2
  continuous provision of 39
  current context 11–28
  emergent *see* emergent literacy
  enhanced provision of 39, 39–40 (case study)
  environment in setting 37
  home-based 118–19
  and listening 38–9
  objects in play environments 120
  phonics' role in 3–4
  practices *see* literacy practices
  roots of 106
  school-based 118–19
  and social disadvantage 42
  and talking 38–9
  variation in home-based 33–4
literacy learning:
  early years provision and 37–43
  and home environment 30–7
  pre-school 19
literacy practices 19–20
  home and nursery comparison (study) 34
  maternal (study) 31–3
  and play (case study) 38
literate:
  becoming 157
  meaning of becoming 18–24

literate environment:
   day-care 67
   in settings 119

mark-making opportunities 138
'Matthew effect' 38–43
meaning, reading for 20
mediating factors for literacy and socioeconomic
   status 42
metacognition:
   definition 91–2
   development in children 92
   elements of 92
   and thinking awareness 92–3
metalinguistic awareness 91
   language play and 99–100
   and reading comprehension (study) 101–2
   and riddles (study) 101–2
   story books and 99
metalinguistic development 90–103
   model (Gombert) 94
   pedagogy principles underpinning (study) 100
metalinguistic knowledge 91
   acquisition 94
   ages and phases 95
   and bilingualism 102–3
   and control bidirectionality 96
   definition 93
   interaction 96–8
   language play and 99–100
   phases of (Gombert's model) 93–4
   and phonics 93, 159
   and phonics precursor 95
   story books and 99
   supporting children's 96–102
midline crossing:
   activities for young children's 86–7
   and learning 77
mind and body connections 76
mind-free body 80
motor skills and readiness for school (study) 81–3
movement-play and neuroscience (study) 79–80
multilingual children, advantages for 6
multimodal literacies 20
music and phonological awareness 151

Nativism 51–2
   limitations 51–2
neuro-motor integration and readiness to learn
   76–7
neuroscience:
   and early years 37
   and movement-play (study) 79–80
non-verbal communication 54
   in English learners 58
notation, invariance of 131
nursery rhymes and reading (study) 143–4

OFSTED inspections and systematic synthetic
   phonics 13

onset–rime:
   meaning 145
   phonological awareness 145
outline of book 8–9

parental involvement:
   in emergent literacy 125–6
   in language learning 69–71
   methods of encouraging 70
   physical activity benefits 88
   in print awareness 125–6
pattern finding in language acquisition 54
pedagogical content knowledge 46, 47
pedagogical skill levels, in setting staff 46
pedagogy:
   of early literacy 43–7
   of phonics 16–17
pencil grip 81
phonemes:
   and graphemes linking 148
   learning activities 153
   meaning 141
   and phonological awareness 152
phonemic awareness 141, 145–8
   acquisition 146
   and analysis of sound 146
   explicit teaching of 153
   language play and 153
   levels of (study) 147
   and phonics 141, 149
   and phonics linked 160
   and phonological awareness 159
   prerequisite for reading 145–6
   and reading correlations (studies) 146–8,
      154–5
   and reading relationship 148
phonics:
   appropriateness 157
   concerns over very young children 18–26
   insufficient for reading 3, 4
   issues in use of 6–7
   and metalinguistic knowledge 93, 159
   necessary for reading 3, 4
   pedagogy of 16–17
   and phonemic awareness 141, 149
   precursors of 159
   and symbolising 130–2
   underpinnings of 26–7
   use of (research review) 4–5
   views on use of 7
phonological awareness 140–55
   activities to develop 149–53
   alliteration and 150
   and dance 151
   development of 142, 142 (fig), 148
   directionality in acquisition of 149
   and language play 150
   and listening 151
   meaning 141
   and music 151

phonological awareness *cont.*
  necessity for reading 149
  onset–rime 145
  pedagogy to support 150
  and phonemes 152
  and phonemic awareness 159
  prerequisite for phonics 148
  rhymes and 143, 150
  and segmenting 152
  and sound 150–1
  and sound effects 151
  syllables 144–5
  and word awareness 150
  words 144
phonological skills, reading and (review) 154–5
physical activity:
  and ADHD (research review) 78–9
  interventions 78–9
  and learning 159
  levels decreasing 83–4
  as literacy 87
  parental involvement 88
physical development:
  activities for young children's 86
  babies 84–6
  and becoming literate 80–3
  learning and 74–88
physical skills:
  immature 78–9
  and learning 78–80
pictures:
  and emergent reading 122 (table)
  symbolic representation 137
  and text *see* text and pictures
play:
  agency in (study) 45
  dynamics of (study) 44–6
  learning through 24–5
  and literacy practices (case study) 38
  symbolic representation 137
  and teaching tensions 25
play environment, literacy opportunities in
  (study) 120
playfulness in interaction 61
playing with language 99–100
pleasure, reading for 20
poverty and literacy 42
practices, literacy *see* literary practices
pre-school literacy learning 19
print:
  books 108–9
  context and recognition 107
  in digital environment 109–10
  and emergent reading 122 (table)
  engagement with 40, 126
  environmental *see* environmental print
  forms and functions 107, 159
  learning about 112–25
  recognition and context 107
  symbolic representation 137

print *cont.*
  understanding is progression 111
  understandings of 110–12
print awareness 106–10
  and bilingual children 113–14
  in digital environment 109–10
  and iPads 109–10
  parental involvement in 125–6
professional knowledge and effective literacy
  teaching 160
proprioception:
  in crawling 85
  developing 85
  immature 78
  and learning 75–6, 80
  and literacy learning 80–1
  meaning 75–6
provision for early literacy:
  adult-focused activity 43
  child-initiated play 43

randomised controlled trials in teaching 23
readiness for school:
  adaptation and 83
  motor skills and (study) 81–3
  tests 82
readiness to learn and neuro-motor integration
  76–7
reading:
  dimensions of 81
  early 81
reading comprehension:
  and metalinguistic awareness (study) 101–2
  and riddles (study) 101–2
reinforcement in language learning 50
representation, meaning 129
research review:
  environmental print and emergent literacy
    107–8
  phonics use 4–5
  phonological skills and reading 154–5
  physical activity and ADHD 78–9
  systematic synthetic phonics 13–14
resources for families 71
rhymes:
  and comprehension 68–9
  and phonological awareness 150
  and reading (study) 143–4
riddles, metalinguistic awareness and 99–100
Risley and Hart (study) 55–6
role play, symbolic representation 137
roots of literacy 106
Rose Review (2006) 13–14
Rosen, Michael:
  book promotion 22
  literacy views 20–1
  testing views 21–2

scaffolding language learning 63
'schoolifying' of early years 26, 43

screening check for six-year-olds in phonics 12,
     15–16
  concerns about 16
  limitations 15
segmenting and phonological awareness 152
Sensorimotor Stage 132
sensory awareness and integration and
     learning 78
shapes, perception of 78
silence:
  as communication 63–4
  in language acquisition 59
Simple View of Reading 14–15, 14 (fig), 68
  flawed 23
  predictions from 15
sitting still 76, 80
social actors, children as (study) 46
social disadvantage and literacy 42
social interaction (study) 55–6
social interactionism 52–3
social practice:
  becoming literate as 19
  literacy as 19–20
society, literacy's role in 2
socioeconomic status:
  and early literacy 41–3
  factors associated with 42
'soft teaching' 31
songs, and comprehension 68–9
sound, and phonological awareness 150–1
sound effects, and phonological awareness 151
spatial orientation to print, development of
     children's 112
speaking and listening as foundation of
     phonics 71–2
spoken language and phonics 159
stimulus-response in language learning 50
stories, importance of 108–9
story books:
  and metalinguistic awareness and
     knowledge 99
  symbolic representation 136–7
story reading 109
  by parents 126
syllables and phonological awareness 144–5
symbolic play 137
symbolic representation:
  and bilingual children 135
  gestures 133, 136
  learning 132–5
  and literary transition 134–5
  mark making 138
  modes 133, 134 (study)
  other symbolic systems 138–9
  pictures 137
  in play 133, 137
  print 137
  role play 137
  sophistication 132

symbolic representation cont.
  of speech 134
  stages of understanding 134–5
  stories and books 136–7
  words 136
symbolic systems, examples of 132
symbolising:
  ability 130
  meaning of 129
  and phonics 130–2
  support activities 136–9
symbolism:
  and literacy 159
  misunderstandings by children (studies) 131
  orders of 130, 138
symbols, and phonics 130
systematic synthetic phonics 2
  and early readers 23–4
  harmful effect 23–4
  method 3, 12
  OFSTED inspections and 13
  prescribed 12–13
  requirements for schemes 17
  review 13–14

talking:
  with babies see babies, talking with
  and literacy 38–9
  opportunities for in provision 64
  sustained 64
teachable moments 62, 97
teaching and play tensions 25
tests, readiness for school 82
text and pictures:
  progression of understanding 111
  understanding of relationship 110–11
thinking awareness, examples of 92–3
thought and language 52
thought processes, stimulating 62
Tomasello on language acquisition 53–4, 55
tummy time:
  benefits of 84
  factors restricting 85
  problems with lack of 84–5

Universal Grammar in language learning 51
usage-based model of language learning 53–4

vision and crawling 85

word awareness, and phonological awareness 150
word reading, and effective reading 101
word recognition, in Simple View of Reading
     14–15
words:
  phonological awareness 144
  symbolic representation 136
writing, iPads support 109, 110
writing systems 113–14